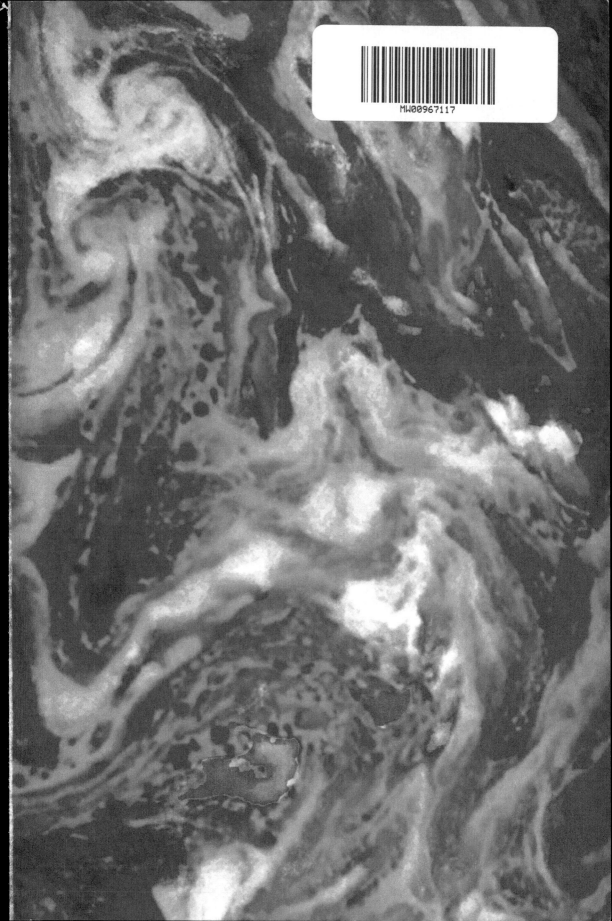

MW00967117

Bobby in his home recording studio
Credit: Toby Talbot

Confessions of
A Marijuana Eater

A Songwriter's Memoir
Bobby Gosh

WIZZIE,
I HOPE YOU ENJOY MY BOOK.

YOUR FRIEND.

Bobby Gosh

8.5.16

RED BARN
BOOK PRODUCTION SERVICES

Shelburne, Vermont

Confessions of a Marijuana Eater
A Songwriter's Memoir
Copyright 2016 Bygosh Music Corporation

All rights reserved. No part of this book may be used or reproduced in any manner
whatsoever without written permission except in the case of brief quotations embodied
in critical articles and reviews.

ISBN: 978-1-944485-11-5

www.bobbygosh.com
www.confessionsofamarijuanaeater.com

Red Barn book production services
Shelburne, Vermont 05482
www.redbarnbooksvt.com

UNCO⌐   ⌐⌐⌐⌐ J

UNCORRECTED

For Billi

Thank you for sharing your life with me.
You are so beautiful.

FOREWORD

Maybe the Book of Genesis got it backwards. Maybe in the beginning all was light. And then the Star Maker said, "Let there be darkness."

The big bang must have been a moment of blinding intensity as everything—space, time, matter, and energy—burst into existence. The universe has been expanding ever since, frantically creating new space as if it somehow fears being confined again. Stars and galaxies wink in and out of existence within the growing void, briefly illuminating small pockets of the cosmos like fireflies on a warm summer night. But darkness prevails and the universe's original radiance slowly fades with time, like a memory or a photograph of what once was.

We're born into this universe with no instruction manual and no obvious answers to life's most profound questions. Why does the world exist? Why am I here? What's the purpose of life?

Many find solace in religion, confident in their belief that a god or gods created and watch over us. Others, however, embark on their own lifelong journey of discovery. As his captivating memoir attests, Bobby Gosh is one of the latter, a student of the universe in search of answers

Because we humans are made of star stuff and governed by the same immutable laws as the farthest galaxy, the answers to our questions may be woven into the very fabric of the universe itself, if only we can find a way to discern them. "Men should take their knowledge from the Sun, the Moon, and the Stars," advised Ralph Waldo Emerson, the famed New England poet and essayist.

But finding a gateway from the quotidian to the cosmic isn't easy, and our rational minds can be a hindrance as much as a help. The ultimate truth of the universe might, as Bobby suggests, "be experienced or known by a feeling, which is impossible to be described and taught with words." It's a view shared by the great Austrian philosopher Ludwig Wittgenstein, among others, who wrote, "There are, indeed, things that cannot be put into words. They make themselves manifest. They are what is mystical."

Meditation, music, religious ceremonies, sensory deprivation, and hallucinogenic substances have been used for ages to reach altered states of consciousness that might provide glimpses into a deeper reality. In 1870, for example, Oliver Wendell Holmes, a prominent Boston physician and poet, inhaled a large quantity of ether—widely used as a surgical anesthetic in those days—in the hope that the universe's secrets would be revealed to his heightened perception. "The veil of eternity was lifted," Holmes later recalled. "The one great truth which underlies all human experience, and is the key to all the mysteries that philosophy has sought in vain to solve, flashed upon me in a sudden revelation."

Many others have also used hallucinogens in a quest for deeper insights. Henry David Thoreau wrote, "If you have an inclination to travel, take the ether. You go beyond the farthest star." The eighteenth-century British chemist Humphrey Davy often inhaled nitrous oxide—laughing gas—under the stars, writing down fragments of poetry and other mystical insights that came into his mind.

Marijuana, a far more natural substance, might also be a bridge to enlightenment, and Bobby is a passionate advocate for its benefits when used wisely. He's not alone. The late Carl Sagan, who inspired me and countless others to become astronomers, smoked marijuana daily to boost his creativity. "Cannabis brings us an awareness that we spend a lifetime being trained to overlook and forget and put out of our minds," he wrote.

Music too has the power to expand consciousness in more subtle ways. Albert Einstein, whose general theory of relativity has been described as the most beautiful theory in the history of science, confessed that if he hadn't been a physicist he probably would have been a musician. "I often think in music," he said. "I live my daydreams in music. I see my life in terms of music."

In a letter to his son Eduard written in 1928, Einstein reflected, "If one hears the angels singing a couple of times during one's life, one can give the world something and one is a particularly fortunate and blessed individual."

Clearly, Bobby Gosh has heard the angels sing. His songwriting and performing have touched millions, and his courage in coming out publicly as both a marijuana user and an atheist will hopefully encourage others to embark on their own unique journey of discovery.

"Follow your bliss and the universe will open doors for you where there were only walls," wrote Joseph Campbell, the great American mythologist. It's a truth that Confessions of a Marijuana Eater and Bobby's remarkable life story reveal in spades.

Michael J. West, Ph.D.

Deputy Director of Science

Lowell Observatory

Flagstaff, Arizona

PREFACE

To quote the Beatle's song, my songwriter's journey was a "long and winding road." I enjoyed every minute of it.

When I was a young boy, my dad told me many times that I was as good as anybody else. I just needed to work harder to be as good or better than others. Because they had failed and returned home, some of my musician friends in my hometown told me I was not good enough to be successful in New York City. I proved them wrong. My career would never have happened, if I had not moved to New York.

Along the way, I had many lucky breaks and what I call "near misses." At times, when I was in over my head, I jumped in regardless and figured out what needed to be done. I am grateful for the many people who believed in me on my journey. They are mentioned in this book.

Early in my career, I discovered marijuana, which I learned how to use safely, and it helped my creativity immensely. Marijuana, one peyote trip, and one LSD trip—among other things—along with careful thought, laid the groundwork that eventually made me a staunch atheist. Marijuana helps me plug my mind into the universe.

With this book, I am coming out of both the marijuana closet and the atheist closet.

I wrote this book for my family, friends, and fans in order to share a complete and honest record of my existence.

I did not become a big star, as I had hoped, but I know that I have become a successful songwriter. That has been enough for me. Most importantly, with marijuana, I have travelled in my mind what seems like millions of miles through the universe, while planted firmly on earth.

I am at peace with what I learned is my insignificant role in the universe. I am grateful for the life I have lived and thankful for my family and friends who joined me along the way.

I am a miniscule part of evolution.

Because this is an unconventional memoir, you may read it in any order you wish: as a collection of short stories and essays or from beginning to end.

ACKNOWLEDGMENTS

I would like to thank the following people for their assistance with my writing efforts for this book:

My wife, Billi, for living my life's story with me; for her editing and proofreading skills; verification of my memories; and constant support for my creative effort.

Denise Shekerjian for giving me a mini-master class in writing; for her early editing help; and for her encouragement that my story was worth writing about. She was there for me every step of the way. Without her help, this book would not be the book it is.

Michael J. West, Ph.D., deputy director of science at Lowell Observatory, Flagstaff, Arizona, for the foreword and his beautiful words.

Marc A. vanderHeyden, Ph.D., a former member of a religious society and president emeritus of Saint Michael's College, for his scholarly mind and for providing an alternative viewpoint to my belief system.

Philip Lamy, Ph.D., professor of sociology and anthropology at Castleton University, for his cannabis insight and belief in my book.

Dr. Joseph McSherry, PhD for kindly sharing his expertise and providing readers with context and historical background of cannabis in the Introduction.

Len Osterberg for his computer expertise, graphic skills, good advice, and for always being available.

Dan Cox for introducing me to Lin Stone.

Lin Stone for guiding me through the complicated world of publishing, with patience and grace.

Gretel Schueller for her editing expertise and content magic.

Greg Forber for graphic design.

CONTENTS

INTRODUCTION

By Joseph W. McSherry, MD, PhD

Cannabis, a dual use plant drug

Nearly three thousand years ago, a shaman was buried in the Gobi desert with two bowls of cannabis—one of the earliest examples of marijuana's long-lived role as a plant drug. More than two thousand years ago, the Greek historian Herodotus described the cannabis-infused rituals of the Scythians: After the death of their leaders, the Scythians set up small tepee-like structures, which they would enter to inhale the fumes of hemp buds thrown onto hot stones—with merry results.

Other plant medicines, such as foxglove (digitalis) and willow bark (aspirin) have a narrow safe range for helping and are poisonous in higher doses; other recreational plant drugs such as tobacco, coffee, and fermented fruits and grains—i.e. alcohol—also are poisons in higher doses. Not so cannabis—well, you may need to sleep it off if you eat too many cookies.

In 1842, an Irish fellow named William Brooke O'Shaughnessy first introduced the miracle drug to Western medicine by way of India. In India, he saw it was helpful in many conditions, from pain relief in rheumatism to stilling the convulsions of infants. Cannabis was soon in the US Pharmacopeia (USP), where the preparation was described, often with alcohol extracts. In the 1920s, with 70-80% alcohol, the preparations were popular for many ailments. In cattle and horses, it was used for colic. All the "Big Pharma" companies of the day had preparations for sale.

So how does it happen that the US DEA now categorizes cannabis as "Schedule I"? That means it has no accepted medical use in the United States and has a high potential for toxicity—a classification that puts cannabis in the same category as heroin and PCP...perhaps it was because it was popular at the wrong time, with the "wrong" people who played the "wrong" music?

Afro-American musicians playing in the bordellos of New Orleans liked marijuana and developed jazz. Around the same time, in 1930, the newly formed Federal Bureau of Narcotics had a budget of $100,000. It desperately needed something to vilify. Opium and cocaine were a small problem, opiate addiction affected 0.5% of the population, and arrests were made mostly by border control. The FBN needed something produced in the USA and widely used. Alcohol was out: Americans of European descent either liked whiskey and fermented fruits and grains, or they were puritanical judges. Both were also members of Congress. In contrast, criminalizing the recreational proclivities of minorities was an easy sell. Wrong, but easy. The FBN called marijuana the "devil weed" and intended to round up the lot of musicians who played bad music—jazz—on marijuana charges in 1947. At the time, the head of the FBN even kept a file called Marijuana and Musicians.

In terms of music and marijuana, when I read the first few lines of Bobby Gosh's memoir it was with particular pleasure that I found another user describing musical notes moving in his head. During a conference I attended in 1971, a neurophysiology researcher stated that one could see notes when listening to Bach fugues. I do not read music, but I have seen the melodies of the Moody Blues passing in waves into the distance. A neuroscience person might call this effect synesthesia. Musicians might call the cause of this effect an assistant. Louis Armstrong called it a friend.

The FBN's effort to round up musicians was eventually cancelled, but in 1951, the Bogg's Act blurred the lines between possession and dealing, cannabis and heroin/cocaine, and established mandatory minimums. By 1952, when Bobby Gosh started touring, the enthusiasm of fighting communism incorporated the view that narcotics came from China and were a tool of the communists to weaken our youth. Bad stuff. Needless to say, Gosh's fear was well justified. Using cannabis was not something one publicized.

Fifteen years later, the college-age children of Americans of European descent coalesced into an anti-establishment, anti-war counterculture force that cared less about communism than about dying for an unpopular war in the jungles of Southeast Asia. Too young to buy alcohol legally, they found cannabis ideal. They also found other young people and people of color from all over the world and different cultures. And they liked music. Think Woodstock.

Music and cannabis thrived. Nevertheless, Nixon's War on Drugs, with the DEA Warriors replacing the Narcs of the FBN, fought on. In 1971, cannabis was eliminated as a medicine when the controlled substances act made cannabis Schedule I; and in 1973, the FBN became the DEA. Property was seized. Zero tolerance was proclaimed. Lots of people were arrested. Lots of damaged people came back from war. The medical benefit to those in pain from injuries and anxiety from the war horrors witnessed could not be denied. Cannabis was available and political lies no longer held it back.

The banditos in the mountains of Columbia found they could make more money if they stuck a brick of cocaine in the bale of cannabis and the rise of the cartels put more professional dealers in place. Then, we had kids with pricy automatic weapons creating death in the streets, although the killing mostly stayed south of the border. And as it has proven impossible to control, ever-harsher rules have been heaped on, culminating in 800,000 arrests per year for cannabis, mostly for possession, and costly, mandatory, minimum incarcerations. And the beat goes on.

Away from the fighting and drug wars, folks not interested in dangerous drugs found they could grow their own. California voted to legalize medical cannabis in 1996. In 1999, the Institute of Medicine found all sorts of potential benefits from cannabis ingestion, just not in favor of smoking. Other states permitted cannabis as medicine in one way or another. A growing number of states have opted to permit cannabis use for non-medical purposes. The War on Drugs machine unravels before our eyes—while the Warriors hope to get their pensions before it is all over.

James Munch, a Professor of Pharmacology at Princeton, and close associate of Harry Anslinger, the former head of the FBN, described the role of cannabis in jazz as lengthening the sense of time, allowing the marijuana-infused musician to put twice as much music between the first note and the second, making good music bad. A curious hypothesis. My 10th grade biology teacher, an MD trained before cannabis stopped being treated as a medicine, described cannabis as a mild hallucinogen that altered time sense.

I am just a neuroscience guy, but I suspect being able to translate auditory images into the visual realm has more to do with musicians and cannabis than the technical ability to play 3/8 beat music to a 3/4 score. My musical abilities are playing vinyl, CDs, and now the internet, so I leave that analysis to musicians.

If you are going to inhale some vapor before reading this memoir, here's a warning:

your sense of passing time will slow. Perhaps you better put on some nice music–a little jazz might be nice, as would some of Bobby Gosh's creations.

Dr. McSherry is a neurologist and widely recognized academic expert on medical cannabis/cannabinoids and its many health benefits. He is also involved in several community service initiatives including his service on the State of Vermont's Marijuana Oversight Committee. Dr. McSherry is the author of numerous academic and public presentations on the medical use of cannabis/cannabinoids in general and as it relates to cancer and other specific medical conditions.

.

I should not talk so much about myself if there were anybody else whom I knew as well.

— Henry David Thoreau

1

CONFESSIONS OF A MARIJUANA EATER

The first time I really got high, I was eighteen years old. Two older musician friends and I were smoking a joint in a parked car. I had puffed marijuana a few times before, but I didn't understand what all the shouting was about. This time was different. It was mind-blowing.

After we finished the joint, we made our way back into the club, where we were performing. As if in a dream, I sat at the piano. I played the first note and instantly thought the song was finished, but I quickly regained control of my mind. Each note I played on the piano had such brilliance and clarity, the likes of which I never heard before. The vibration of every note pulsed through me. I saw the notes and chords dancing and moving within my head. They took on a luminous, otherworldly character.

To my ears, we sounded like a symphony orchestra. I had an incredible feeling of euphoria and all-knowing. I felt so connected to every note that I was able to improvise new ways of playing the song. Because all three of us were high, we were so in tune with each other that we seemed to be playing with one mind. This was the first time I understood what getting high felt like—and I loved it. I sensed that the audience was feeling our excitement, paying extra attention to our performance, and thoroughly enjoying it. Little did I know that marijuana was to become my creative companion for the rest of my life. After I moved to New York City, marijuana helped me tune into the pop music scene of the 1970s; it helped me come up with my own style of songwriting.

Along the way, I was fortunate to meet, write songs with, and perform with many greats of the music world, including legendary lyric writer Sammy Cahn, Paul Anka, Frank Sinatra, Barbra Streisand, and Billy Joel. The very first voice to record "My Way," Frank Sinatra's signature song, was, in fact, mine. I've been fortunate to have had a successful career; and the joys of marijuana are woven through the fabric of my life, feeding my creativity.

Nowadays, hearing that a pop musician smoked or ate pot probably wouldn't make front-page news. But I was born in 1936, the same year the anti-marijuana propaganda movie *Reefer Madness* debuted. I grew up in a time when fear and paranoia toward marijuana were widespread and the possession of a simple joint could land you serious jail time and destroy a career. Robert Mitchum, the actor, did jail time and suffered damage to his image when he was arrested for possession of one joint.

I began writing this book more than forty years ago. It was to be a book about marijuana usage. At that time, I had almost twenty years' experience using marijuana. Life, family, and work put my book project on hold. For the past few years, I entertained the idea of writing about my "life's ride." As I began to write about my "ride," the original idea for the marijuana book and the new idea merged.

Today, the general public's perception of marijuana is similar to what it was back then. I recently met a woman from Colorado. I asked her, "What do you think about your state's legalization of marijuana?" She answered simply, "It fries your brain." That sounds to me like shades of *Reefer Madness* and Nancy Reagan's "Just Say No" failed antidrug campaign.

True, there are legal medical marijuana clinics in at least twenty-three states as of this writing, though they are not legal in the eyes of the federal government. In many states, possession of less than an ounce of marijuana is tantamount to a traffic ticket. In Illinois, possession of up to 15 grams (approximately one half ounce) is subject to a $125 fine. In 2012 the states of Washington and Colorado voted to legalize marijuana, and in 2014 Alaska and Oregon joined them. In February 2015 it became legal to grow up to six plants indoors only for personal use in Washington, D.C. You are allowed to possess up to two ounces and give away up to one ounce as a gift. Selling it is illegal. In New York State medical clinics are only allowed to sell liquid or oil extracts, drops, vapors, and capsules; products for conventional smoking cannot be legally sold in clinics. Some other states allow you to grow a few plants for personal use. Growing marijuana takes skill, knowledge, and time to get decent product. I would rather buy marijuana legally than go through all the complications of growing it, though I like having the option. More states are now considering various forms of the legalization of medical and recreational marijuana, including Vermont.

There have been few gains toward the general public's true understanding of what marijuana does and could do for society, but this is beginning to improve rapidly. The states that legalized marijuana quickly learned that there are many hurdles to overcome. Colorado, the first state to go legal, made a serious initial error by underestimating all the problems associated with edible marijuana, especially concerning children. There are no standards of potency for any type or amount of marijuana purchased on the black market, except for the "medical marijuana black market," which has arisen due to the lack of safeguards and enforcement about how much can be bought by an individual in different states. You are on your own as far as knowing how high you are going to get from the unknown potency and purity of what you are consuming. That's sort of like taking pills from your medicine cabinet, mixing them together, popping a handful into your mouth, and waiting to see what happens.

It is time for all marijuana users to come out of the closet. In this way, society can begin to treat marijuana the same way we treat alcohol and tobacco. It needs to be regulated for safety. With this book, I am coming out of the marijuana closet.

I can only write if I tell the truth about my experiences with drugs. So, I will now confess and come clean: I have consumed marijuana, off and on, for more than sixty years. In the late fifties, sixties, and early seventies, I smoked it moderately, but hated the smoking part because I didn't smoke cigarettes. From the mid-seventies on, I have baked marijuana cookies and found that to be my ideal method for delivering the plant to my system. I believe that marijuana should only be ingested and never smoked. Smoking anything could eventually kill you, and at the very least, is not healthy for your lungs.

At times I have gone for years without using marijuana and have, in my case, not found it to be habit-forming or addictive. I never bought cocaine, but consumed it when offered on occasion in the seventies and eighties and enjoyed it. I used fresh peyote and LSD each only once in the eighties, both of which caused mind-blowing hallucinations. I also tried hashish and mushrooms in the early years. These incidents are woven throughout my life and many of them are described in this book. I have never regretted even one minute of it. Marijuana has fed my creative juices immensely over my professional life in music. In contrast, I have consumed alcohol since the age of sixteen and never felt that it aided me creatively. For the past decade, other than an occasional glass of great wine, I have basically stopped consuming alcohol.

I believe that marijuana is a miracle drug like aspirin, only much more powerful. It's a weed so it should be cheap and legal like aspirin, but the government makes it illegal. As a result, it becomes very expensive, and requiring the government to build prisons to house the lawbreakers. Criminals get involved because of the enormous tax-free profits they can make.

According to a cover story on marijuana in the June 3, 2013, issue of *Barron's* (a financial magazine), if the government legalized marijuana, "it would hurt Mexican drug cartels, raise billions in tax revenue for ailing states, and lighten the burden on our police and prisons." Keeping marijuana illegal makes millionaires out of criminals and criminals out of users.

Keeping marijuana illegal also helps the drug companies. According to the online site *Expressions of Truth*, "Marijuana has been found to suppress cancer, reduce blood pressure, treat glaucoma, alleviate pain, eliminate nausea, and even inhibit HIV. It is an antioxidant, anti-inflammatory, and neuroprotective. Cannabis is one of the most powerful healing plants on the planet." It can increase appetite in cancer patients and enhance the taste of food. What drug company would want to compete with all of this? It has been said that marijuana is the safest therapeutic substance known to man.

The negative health effect of smoking marijuana is the biggest downside to using the drug. This can easily be remedied by simply ingesting it. Cookies, brownies, candies, pastries, beverages, lozenges, tinctures, oils, and capsules are just a few of the methods of delivering marijuana into your system without smoking it. Yet all you hear about in the media is smoking the weed.

Ingesting marijuana, however, is not for amateurs. All edible products must be clearly labeled with the potency of each individual serving. A warning (like a marijuana leaf) must also be clearly marked on the label, stating exactly how much a beginner can take to avoid paranoia and hallucinations. Potency affects people differently according to their experience with the drug and their body type. Educational materials must be handed out liberally wherever marijuana is sold. There should be a universal federal rating system for users: something like beginner, intermediate, and expert. There should be a standard for the percentage of THC in any given dose of edible or cigarette. There should be a recommendation on the label as to how much of the dose should be used by the beginner, intermediate, or expert. The presence of a certain level of THC in the blood does not correlate predictably with a level of impairment. All edible products must also be in childproof packaging. Each serving of edible pot should be individually wrapped. A beginner must be instructed to proceed cautiously.

The logistics of legalization are a learning experience and mistakes will be made, as in Colorado. I cannot overestimate the need for a simple instruction manual for the beginning marijuana eater. My book is not that manual, but it is a little more information. The needed manual must be fully researched by the federal or state governments—and/or legal growers and sellers—similar to the printed information you receive with any doctor's prescription.

I believe that the time has come for society to be truthful about what marijuana really is and what it does to and for the user. We legally allow alcohol and cigarettes and prescription drugs to kill people, yet at the same time we sweep the useful and relatively harmless marijuana under the rug of illegality.

Prescription opioid painkillers, such as OxyContin, oxycodone, hydrocodone, and Fentanyl, are responsible for more overdose deaths than heroin and cocaine combined. In May 2014, the World Health Organization reported that alcohol kills one person every ten seconds. On the other hand, there is basically no record of marijuana killing anyone.

Other than telling my story, I hope my experience with marijuana helps to inform anyone who is negative toward the drug, to help them understand that marijuana is not a gateway drug any more than alcohol. When used intelligently, it is much safer and more rewarding than alcohol. As Clarence Page, a Chicago journalist, said, "Every heroin addict started by drinking milk." I'm not telling anyone to do marijuana, but if you do decide to try it, in my opinion, eating it is the only way to go.

I believe marijuana is no more addictive than chocolate. What I'm trying to say here is: Do not judge me—a moderate user of marijuana—as some kind of drug addict, any more than you would call the moderate social drinker an alcoholic. I hope my friends and the readers who do not know me will give me the same consideration as that they would give to a moderate social drinker.

I let how I lived my life speak for itself. I always told my children, "I will never punish you for what you did, just always tell me the truth." I am a respectable and responsible person and a caring parent. Instead of a few glasses of wine at cocktail hour, I may choose to ingest a controlled dose of marijuana in a cookie. My situation, as a moderate marijuana eater, is similar to someone who was gay and in the closet a decade or more ago. You cannot talk freely about using marijuana without being judged by many people. Many of my closest friends don't know of my marijuana usage. I don't know what they will think of me if they read this book, but I do trust that they will know who I am. That's why I decided to come out of the marijuana closet. I hope I might encourage other marijuana users to come out of the closet so that, one day soon, marijuana is perceived no differently than alcohol or tobacco.

It's time that the hypocrisy of how society deals with marijuana is discussed and acted upon in a truthful, intelligent, and legal manner. To quote a cover story about the business of marijuana in the October 29, 2012, issue of *Newsweek*: "Herbal cannabis can be regulated, taxed, and safely sold." I would add that it also can be safely ingested. I can't think of a better way for state and federal governments to raise much-needed new taxes. I suggest we regulate the sale of the less harmful marijuana the same as cigarettes and alcohol. This would eliminate the black market, empty many prison cells, and free up much needed police time for more productive uses. At the time of this writing, you can still get a life sentence for certain marijuana convictions in Texas . At least 750,000 people are arrested each year on marijuana charges.

The present trend toward decriminalization, legalization, and medical marijuana clinics should decrease these numbers immensely in the coming years. However, the price of legal marijuana, including taxes, must be no higher than black market marijuana, or the black market will still exist.

A final example that illustrates how the general public presently views the subject of marijuana: A subscription to *High Times*, the forty-year-old, excellent marijuana magazine, is still mailed in a plain wrapper just like adult magazines, and is placed on the newsstand's top shelf next to *Penthouse* and *Hustler*.

2

EARLIEST RECOLLECTIONS

My dad, Hans Heinrich Gosch, came to the United States in 1927 from Germany with the help of a relative who owned a knitting factory. When he arrived at Ellis Island, Dad had a coin worth 50 million German marks in his pocket. But it was worthless. People walked down the street in Germany with wheelbarrows full of money. Inflation was so bad that the beautifully engraved, gold-colored coin couldn't purchase a loaf of bread. The factory in Wyomissing, Pennsylvania, went out of business during the late depression and my dad, a machinist who had repaired the knitting machines, was laid off. Feeling sorry for my dad's situation, the relative, who had offices in the Empire State Building in better times, allowed us to live rent free on an abandoned farm he owned in Womelsdorf. My parents had no income or money saved. My mother, whose maiden name was Margaret May Zeller, was Pennsylvania Dutch.

My earliest recollection is of Christmas Eve, 1941, in the farmhouse. I was five and a half years old and too excited to sleep. I stood on the stairs and saw my parents crying at the kitchen table with their arms wrapped around each other. I heard them say there was no money for Christmas presents for my younger brother and me. My brother Fred was born that previous March.

Because money was tight, during spring and summer one of our staple foods was frog legs. Dad would come home after a day of looking for a job, grab his 22-caliber rifle, and shoot a mess of frogs in the creek by our house for dinner. The creek ran through the basement. I would sit on the cellar steps and fish for the trout that occasionally swam through. If I got lucky, we would have fish for dinner. Sometimes I would let the fishing rod lie securely on the cellar steps and later return to find a fish on the hook.

At one dinner I asked my parents what the strange meat was that we were eating and got no immediate answer. I leaped up from the table and ran out to the barn to discover that my pet rabbit had disappeared from his cage.

There was another pet incident from this time that influenced me for the rest of my life. I could never shake it from my memory. Our dog disappeared one day, so Dad and I went searching for him. We found him on the nearby main road. One half of him was on one side of the road, and the other half was on the other side.

After the rabbit and dog experiences, I always hesitated to get attached to animals later in life, except for our family dog, Samantha. She was given to me as a surprise birthday present by our children when they were young.

Another lifelong fear, formed early, concerns motorcycles. One rainy night in the early forties, I was leaning on my arms in the back seat of Dad's 1936 Pontiac (bought new in better days for $800) looking out the rear window at a motorcycle riding behind us. The bike got caught in the trolley tracks and the rider was thrown off. Dad stopped the car and we got out. The rider was dead and the footrest was caught in the track.

We watched the bike spin uncontrollably in circles for about a half hour until it ran out of gas. I have had a fear of motorcycles ever since that night.

In 1942 Dad found a job in Reading, Pennsylvania, at a small machine shop owned by a German named Karl Liebernecht. They made parts for airplane engines for the war effort. My parents, now having an income, rented a house in Reading, about thirty miles from the farmhouse.

In the middle of World War II, Dad lost his job at the machine shop. The longer you worked there, the more job seniority you earned. A person with less seniority than you could not take your job unless you quit or did something wrong. Some guy under Dad wanted his job, so he told a boss that he saw Dad saluting Hitler in the locker room. Ironically, Dad had left Germany to get away from Hitler because he saw what was coming. He was a loyal American citizen but still lost his job.

The next day, Dad went to the local FBI office in Reading and asked to be investigated in order to get his job back. The agent in charge said that he had already been investigated, as were all the employees at Karl Liebernecht's shop because the owner was of German nationality. The agent told Dad he was cleared, but the FBI could not get his job back. He tried to enlist in the army, but was rejected as 4F for flat feet. Shortly thereafter, he got a job at Luden's Cough Drop factory in Reading, repairing machines. Dad worked at Luden's for the rest of his life, until he died at the age of 63.

Dad was a hard-working, responsible, and dependable nice guy. He and my mom were good parents with very simple tastes. Off and on throughout my youth, Mom would work at a cheese counter in a local farmer's market to bring in some extra income. I could usually tell Mom was home from work because of the smell of cheese that permeated the house. She was an excellent cook, specializing in Pennsylvania Dutch recipes. For about five years, Mom worked as a cook in Joe's Restaurant in Reading. Joe Sznarecki was an internationally-known wild mushroom expert. His restaurant drew clientele from around the world. Mom was trusted with making Joe's five mushroom soup. Sometimes she would bring leftovers home for a special treat for the family. To this day I love wild mushrooms, especially morels.

Mom was a proficient pianist who could read music and also play "by ear" (without sheet music). She could rip off a lively version of "Malaguena" or "Tico Tico," two popular songs of the day.

Dad and Mom were very fair in dealing with my brother Fred and me. If we stepped out of line, however, Dad was quick to discipline us. He made a wooden paddle, which would be used occasionally, and if it was not handy, he used his belt. One time, Dad bent me over and the paddle hit a bone at the base of my spine. It made a hollow *boing* sound, which shocked and scared both of us. He never spanked Fred or me again.

Dad and Mom were not big drinkers, but enjoyed going to a local bar or German club for a few beers, whenever possible. This was their social life. They had two or three couples with whom they were good friends. One thing about my Dad: If a friend ever crossed him, in any way, he would dismiss that person for the rest of his life.

Mom and Dad always encouraged my music career, and took great pride in my accomplishments for the rest of their lives. Neither of them ever told me *I love you* until very late in their lives, but I always knew they did.

When we moved to Reading in 1942, I was six years old. There were trolley tracks in front of our house at 1661 North 10th Street. We were the last stop; the trolley storage barn was across the street. I became a member of the neighborhood gang and the nickname they gave me was "Horseshit" because I moved there from a farm.

Our gang would take bottle caps, remove the cork, put in tipped matchstick heads, and replace the cork. We then put these "bombs" on the trolley tracks and waited patiently for the next trolley to explode them. We lived two doors away from a corner bar. Dad made me a shoeshine kit and I would shine shoes for 10 cents. I still have the kit today. An ice cream wagon, drawn by a horse, would stop in front of our house every early evening. My usual order was a Cho Cho, an upside-down, Dixie-Cup-shaped mocha popsicle on a stick. As I ate my ice cream, I would smell the deposits the horse would almost always leave on the street in front of our house. To this day, I can still smell them.

On Saturdays my parents would give me twenty-five cents to go to the movies with my friends. The eleven-cent ticket would cover the afternoon double feature, which was preceded by a few serials like "The Lone Ranger." The remainder of the money was for trolley fare. I would walk instead so I could spend the fare money on candy.

The worst thing our gang ever did was to steal car batteries from the local junkyard. My other nickname was "Brains" and I would be consulted on such matters. We stole the batteries from the junkyard at night. The plan was to resell them back the next day to the cranky old junk dealer for seventy-five cents each. I thought it was a bad idea but was overruled. The next day, when we took a wagonload of his batteries back to him on a red Radio Flyer, he was on to us immediately. He said he would report us to the police, the junkyard dog barked ferociously, and we hightailed it out of there, leaving behind the wagon of batteries.

When I was thirteen years old, Dad gave me the beautiful, gold-colored German coin, dated 1923—the same one that was in his pocket when he came to America. It is heavy and larger than a silver dollar. Engraved on it is *50 millionen Mk.* (50 million German marks). Dad said, when he left Germany, it was worth about eleven cents. I still have the coin in my change dish today. It constantly reminds me of the dangers of inflation as the world's governments toy with the economy, all the while ignoring the fact that history repeats itself.

3

THE MUSIC BEGINS

I was six years old and in first grade when my parents arranged piano lessons for me. They were both amateur musicians. Dad played saxophone and violin and my mother played the piano. Dad sold his sax and violin during the farm days so that we could eat. My piano teacher, an old maid named Mary Deeter, drove to our house weekly in her Chevrolet coupe. She charged fifty cents a lesson. She was a competent classical pianist and a very strict teacher. The only downside I remember was that she always had bad breath.

My parents made me consistently practice one hour a day. Many days, the gang would stand outside our house and yell, "Hey Horsie, come out and play." But I would have to stay inside and practice on the old upright piano.

After five years of lessons, Miss Deeter raised her fee to one dollar a lesson. I was becoming lax in my piano practicing, so Dad said I would either have to start taking my practicing seriously or quit the lessons. I was in the fifth grade at the time and had begun playing the piano at school, as the students marched into assembly. I noticed that I was doing something sort of special and some of the girls were paying attention to me. So I decided to apply myself to practicing and continue my piano lessons, even though I later flunked music in sixth grade.

When I was thirteen and in the seventh grade, our family had to move in with my grandparents on my mother's side for a year. It was 1949 and returning war veterans were given housing preferences. My Dad could not find a house to rent. My grandparents, Gertrude and Harry Zeller, lived in a fairly large Sears and Roebuck mail-order house they had built in Stouchsburg, Pennsylvania, the little town where I was born. A huge copper cistern that collected rainwater from the roof for the toilet and bathing encompassed one large room on the second floor. The water was strictly rationed, so there was also an outhouse.

If we were going to have chicken for dinner, my grandfather Zeller would grab a few chickens from the coop and chop their heads off. I can still picture the headless chickens flopping around the yard before they died. Then they had to be scalded so the feathers could easily be plucked.

My mother's brother George, his wife, and my great-grandmother, Minnie Stoltz, also lived in the house. Before Minnie's husband died and before she moved in with us, I remember three things: Her house had a hand pump for water in the kitchen. There was always a huge bowl of saffron, which she grew, drying on the window sill. And, I was completely fascinated by how my great-grandfather Stoltz ate his peas. He would balance peas single file on the entire blade of a table knife, lift it carefully to his mouth, and let the peas roll one by one into their final destination without spilling a single one. No matter how I tried, I could never master this feat.

There were double front parlors in my grandparents' house, which was the style of the day. Each one contained an upright piano for me to practice on. My grandfather Zeller was a professional house painter, so the house was always meticulously maintained, inside and out.

A few years after we moved out of the house, my other great-grandmother, Zeller, became very ill. She was moved into the house, where she was bedridden twenty-four hours a day in one of the front parlors, which was converted into a bedroom. Standing outside the parlor bedroom, I could hear my grandparents talking seriously with the doctor about her condition. I believe they called it senility, the name given at that time to very advanced Alzheimer's patients.

I remember witnessing grandmother Zeller conducting a sort of "powwow" and healing ceremony for her. Although she was Pennsylvania Dutch, grandmother Zeller spoke some sort of special words or incantations over her mother-in-law's unconscious body. It didn't work. Later in life, I would come to realize it could never have worked. Today, as an atheist, I would classify powwow as wishful thinking, the same as prayer. A short time after that, the doctor came to the house, injected my great-grandmother Zeller with a drug, and she died. I guess it could be called a mercy killing or assisted suicide.

While living with my grandparents, I also had my first experience with religion. My parents did not go to church, but my grandparents devotedly attended church every Sunday. To humor my grandparents, my mother and I would join them. Dad never went. My grandfather was a deacon or something, and he never missed a week. He wore twenty-seven medals on a chain awarded to him for perfect attendance for twenty-seven years. The impressive array of jewelry almost reached the floor.

I enjoyed singing in church and my grandmother told me I had a "nice singing voice." I noticed, however, that after the service, the women would divide into groups in the parking lot. I'd overhear them saying things like "That hat looks terrible on her." Or "How can they afford a car like that?" I noticed how quickly the "parking lot hypocrites" forgot what they had just learned in church.

After a few months, I refused to go to church, much to my grandparents' dismay. This experience laid the groundwork for my becoming an atheist later in life.

After ten years of strictly classical piano lessons, Miss Deeter died. I was now a sixteen-year-old competent classical pianist with a memorized repertoire of pieces from Grieg's Piano Concerto in A minor, op. 16 to Gershwin's "Rhapsody In Blue." Miss Deeter would not allow me to play popular songs, but I cheated. At the age of fourteen, Dad got me a job playing piano for three hours every Saturday night at a local bar three blocks from our house. They paid me eight dollars per night and for the first week or two, I only had sheet music for about five popular songs. One of them was Tony Bennett's first big hit, "Cold, Cold Heart," written by Hank Williams. I filled in the five popular songs with my showy classical works. I bought more sheet music to expand my popular repertoire. Dad was very proud of me. He would sit at the bar, waiting for me to finish work as he got quietly plastered. When Miss Deeter came to give me a lesson, I hid the popular song sheet music.

After she died, I began lessons with Ralph Tragel, the best jazz pianist in town. He taught me harmony, the circle of fifths, and how to fake songs—meaning how to play a song by ear without sheet music. After a year and a half of lessons, Mr. Tragel told me he taught me everything he knew and I was now on my own.

I was a senior in high school, playing with local bands on weekends, and with the best musicians in Reading, a city of 100,000 people. In one band, I accompanied a very good African American female jazz singer at a place called The Melody Bar. It also didn't hurt that she could have passed for Whitney Houston today. The bandstand, which rotated, was in the center of a large circular bar. The band leader, Frankie Scott, taught me how to play behind the singer, to feed her the chords, and otherwise stay out of her way. I decided I wanted to do more. I wanted to both sing and accompany myself on the piano.

Singing while playing the piano requires a certain type of coordination. Accompanying another singer while you play piano is fairly easy because you are doing only one thing. But when you back up your own voice by also playing the piano, you are concentrating on two entirely different jobs. It is a skill you can only acquire after considerable experience doing it. It's sort of like patting your head and rubbing your stomach at the same time.

But it came naturally to me. Just as I would feed the chords to the singer I was accompanying, I learned to feed the chords to myself and think as a singer while doing it. You are totally in control of both jobs. In contrast, a singer needs to work with a separate pianist. As a singer-pianist you have an advantage. It was an important breakthrough for me, allowing me to make a living singing and playing piano, by myself, whenever needed.

I also played with a trio at an afterhours club with the nickname "The Bucket of Blood." (The club earned this dubious distinction when a customer was stabbed to death at the bar.) I played an old, upright piano with some missing keys. The leader of the trio was a sixty-year-old, hard-drinking upright bass player named Jazz Weist. One night he told me about a guy he knew who just bought a house with five bathrooms. Jazz said, "I knew he was full of crap, but I didn't know he was that full of crap." Remembering that quote has made me laugh many times throughout my life.

By this time I was quite familiar with drinking alcohol, but was fairly conservative about how much I would drink. One night, however, I was out drinking at a local bar with some musician friends and ended up drunk on the bathroom floor, a few feet from the urinal. My friends took me home and the next morning I vowed never to drink too much ever again. After that experience, I could always gauge when I drank enough and would stop before I was drunk.

In 1954, now a senior in high school, I would occasionally drive to New York City on weekends with a musician friend to listen to the top jazz musicians of the day. We would stay at the President Hotel on 48th Street off Times Square for two dollars a night each. We would eat all our meals at Romeo's spaghetti joint on Times Square. A large plate of spaghetti was 35 cents with a roll, 65 cents if you added meatballs. We would go to Birdland on Broadway around 50th Street, where a typical show would be Stan Kenton's big band, saxophonist Stan Getz's quartet, and pianists Art Tatum or Bud Powell. After standing at the bar with a few 75-cent beers and watching and hearing all three acts, we would go next door to the Band Box. There a typical bill would be Maynard Ferguson's big band, the Gerry Mulligan Quartet with Chet Baker, and The Dave Brubeck Quartet. If you sat at the bar, where there was no cover charge, all it would cost was a few bucks for beer. It was truly amazing to see and hear all these jazz greats. It was also very inspirational. Because I was aspiring to be a jazz musician at that point, I learned a lot by listening to them play.

Nights usually ended at the Hickory House on 52nd Street to listen to the pianist Billy Taylor and his trio, and then down to Greenwich Village to catch Thelonious Monk in the late show at the Five Spot.

Some nights we would go to the Metropole at 48th Street and 7th Avenue and hear Woody Herman and his big band at the time, the Third Herd. The Metropole was a narrow room an entire block long, with a bar running the whole length of the place. Behind the bar was a narrow ledge with only enough depth for one musician to stand. The big bands of seventeen men or more would line up next to each other on the ledge behind the bar, stretching out at least fifty feet. For the price of a beer, you could stand at the middle of the bar and have the mind-blowing experience of hearing some of the best big bands in the country. Stan Kenton, Maynard Ferguson, Woody Herman, and Count Basie all played there. It was the ultimate stereo experience.

In 1954, I got a call from Tony Pellegrino, a local saxophone player, asking if I wanted to join a big band and go out on the road for a summer tour. Reading was known as a city full of good musicians and Tony was asked by a Philadelphia orchestra leader named Larry Fotine to assemble a band for a road tour. The band would be accompanying the singer Kitty Kallen, who that summer had two hit songs on the national top ten music charts. I accepted the job. We traveled in cars and toured the eastern part of the country for the entire summer. I was 18 years old and had just graduated high school. I was in musical paradise.

We played in places like the Steel Pier in Atlantic City and Brighton Beach in Brooklyn, along with many amusement parks and dance halls. Kitty Kallen drew the crowds because of her two hits, "Little Things Mean a Lot" and "In the Chapel in the Moonlight." Both songs were on the same 45-rpm record. One song hit for her and the radio disc jockeys turned the record over and made the second side a hit also. That is probably the only time in recording history that two hits were on one single 45-rpm record.

The rest of the musicians in the band were from about thirty to sixty years old. I was the youngster. Needless to say, I got a great education about alcohol and drugs on that tour. I recall drinking alcohol on the tour and observing the marijuana use going on with some members of the band. I did take a few hits of the drug, but I didn't consume enough marijuana to experience getting really high. I approached it conservatively because the band leader, Larry Fotine, was very square and adamantly against drug use. Getting caught with marijuana anywhere at that time was an extremely serious offense.

As I said earlier, the actor Robert Mitchum made national headlines in the late 1940s, when he was caught with one marijuana joint and did prison time. A musician friend of mine from Reading, Dick Hafer, got caught with some marijuana while playing saxophone with Woody Herman's band in the Midwest in the 1950s, and his arrest was in the newspapers nationwide. So on the tour, I approached smoking marijuana very cautiously, fearing the serious consequences of getting caught with the drug.

Toward the end of the tour, Dad sent me a telegram stating that Albright College, a liberal arts college in Reading, offered me a 50 percent scholarship to attend the college for four years; it would begin with the upcoming fall semester. The scholarship was for being in the National Honor Society and in the top 10 percent of my high school senior class of over 800 students. Because everyone was telling me I would never make a good living as a musician, I took Albright up on the offer. My total cost for the four years to get a B.S. in economics was $2,500.

While attending college as a day student and living with my parents, I formed a trio with a saxophone player, Guy Sheaffer, and an upright bass player, Art Mease. After a year or so, Al Jacobson replaced Guy on sax and stand-up drums. We worked for a few years at a local bar and restaurant, the Woodward Cafe. I transcribed all the vocal arrangements of the Four Freshmen, a popular singing group at the time, and the three of us did a good job of sounding like them. The owners of the cafe, another friend, and I decided to book the Four Freshmen into a large theater in Reading. We would promote the concert and hopefully make some money. The evening of the concert in March was greeted by a huge snowstorm, so many people could not get there. The theater wasn't even half full. My friend talked the Four Freshmen into taking a greatly reduced price for the concert, so we took only a moderate financial hit on the evening. After the concert, the Four Freshmen came to the cafe, where my trio was playing. Upon walking into the cafe, and hearing us imitating their sound, the Four Freshmen said unanimously, "Man, that's us singing." I guess we weren't too bad.

It was at the Woodward Cafe, where I had my first really positive experience with marijuana as described in the first chapter of this book. Al and Art, both being at least fifteen or twenty years older than me, introduced me to the real joys and powers of marijuana—even though I did not like putting the smoke in my lungs. I had tried smoking for a few months when I was eight. A friend supplied our gang with cigarettes that he stole from his father's store. I never liked smoking the Victory and Kool cigarettes he gave me and only did it to retain my reputation in the gang. One day my Dad caught me smoking, flushed the cigarettes down the toilet, and that was the end of that. I quit smoking cigarettes at the age of eight!

Mom and Dad never knew I used marijuana. If they would have found out, I really believe they would not have thought it was a big deal, because they always trusted my judgment.

4

BILLI

One night while playing at the Woodward Cafe, a girlfriend of Al's came into the club with another girl, Billi Williams. They were both very popular students at Albright. I knew them from seeing them around the campus. Since I was a day student, I went to class and then headed straight for home. I didn't participate in any campus activities and had no interest in college life. I accelerated my credits so that I could graduate in three and a half years. I was there only to earn a degree, as a backup if the music business didn't pan out.

Al and I sat with his girlfriend and Billi during an intermission. Billi and I hit it off immediately. But she said she had to leave in order to get back on campus before her 11:00 P.M. curfew. "Had she ever sneaked out of the dorm?" I asked. She said, "No." I invited her to a jam session at an afterhours club where some jazz musicians gathered after their regular gigs. We decided I would drive to the dorm and wait outside. If the venetian blinds were closed, it meant that she failed to get out. If they were open, she'd be hiding in the bushes and meet me at the car. The blinds were open! Billi got into my Triumph TR3, and we spent the rest of the night at the club. After breakfast at a local diner, Billi went into the ladies room to change into her waitress uniform, which she had in her pocketbook. I drove her directly to the college dining hall, where she had a job serving breakfast to the students.

At the time I had been engaged to a girl, Joan Hunt, for a few years, but things were not going well. She didn't like me working nights as a musician. One week after I met Billi at the Woodward Cafe, I broke the engagement. One week later, I introduced Billi to my parents. Billi was pinned to a former Albright student who was away at medical school. They had an arrangement that they could both date other people while apart. Big mistake for her boyfriend. Lucky break for me.

I graduated early in January 1958 and Billi followed soon after in May 1958. Around the time of her graduation, Billi returned the pin to her former boyfriend. He later married Billi's best friend, who seemed to be waiting in the wings. I found out many years later that Joan Hunt was tragically murdered by her mentally ill son.

Billi, originally from Upper Montclair, New Jersey, stayed in Reading after graduation and got a job teaching in an elementary school in Blue Ball, Pennsylvania. In order to supplement my music income, I sold Electrolux vacuum cleaners on the side. I would sell cleaners on my way to pick her up after teaching, as she didn't have a car. One day I stopped at an Amish home. I sprinkled dirt on the floor to demonstrate the power of the Electrolux. I asked the lady of the house where I could plug in the cleaner. She informed me, "We don't have electricity." I cleaned up my mess and hightailed it out of there.

The next year, Billi began teaching first grade in Reading. I got a job playing piano and singing in the town's most expensive and classiest restaurant, Stokesay. Built in the 1920s by a wealthy industrialist, it was a reproduction of a castle in Shropshire, England. My salary for performing six nights a week was $125. It included a room and all my meals, which made it a very good deal. Since graduating and leaving my parents' home, I had been living in an apartment. I left that and moved into a very nice room over the gate house entryway at Stokesay. Billi got an apartment in Reading and I moved in with her. The room at Stokesay was hardly used, but served as a good cover for our living together illicitly.

We got married on February 28, 1959, and had the reception at Stokesay. For our honeymoon, we drove through a snow storm to Fort Lauderdale in our blue Triumph TR3 with the side curtains. While we were in Florida, a friend and his family reserved a table by the stage for Frank Sinatra's show at the Fontainebleau Hotel in Miami Beach. They invited Billi and me to be their guests. We both loved Sinatra, so we were having a really good time. At one point during the show, I said to our guests at the table, "I'll bet my new bride Billi is the only woman in this room that Sinatra couldn't screw." Billi immediately popped up and said, "Don't put any money on it."

After our honeymoon, I had fifty-seven cents left in my pocket. On the way back we got a ticket in a speed trap in Georgia. The policeman told us to follow him to a billboard outside of town. Behind the billboard, a guy was sitting at a small desk. He fined us $125 and demanded cash or he would put me in jail. The next day, we had to buy a new battery for the Triumph. We had $400 in the bank from wedding gifts. That and a few pieces of cheap furniture were all we had, except for each other.

Well—and a notice from my draft board, which was waiting in the mail when we returned from our honeymoon. I would be drafted into the army in thirty days, unless I joined the army reserve. I chose six months active duty in the reserves followed by six more years of weekend monthly meetings and two weeks of summer training camp each year. Six weeks after our wedding, I left for basic training at Fort Knox in Kentucky. I arrived at 3:00 A.M. and they woke us up at 5:00 A.M for calisthenics. We went to breakfast. I ate a greasy, disgusting meal, and then I walked outside the mess hall and promptly threw up.

It felt like I was in prison. I missed Billi very much and wrote my first love song ever, a love song for her. It was titled "One Never Knows." It was a good first attempt, but certainly not capable of becoming a hit song. After nine weeks of basic training, I got a weekend pass and Billi flew down to Fort Knox to be with me. My bunk mate, Buel Goodin, lived nearby in Louisville and invited Billi and me to stay with him and his wife in their home. Billi and I stayed in the bedroom for twenty-four hours, except for coming out for a dinner of southern fried chicken, which Buel's wife graciously cooked. We had to confess to them that we broke the bed. They said, "Don't worry, it has happened before."

Shortly after that, I was transferred to Fort Gordon in Augusta, Georgia. On my first weekend pass, I walked into the bar at the Bon Air Hotel, which was at the Augusta National Golf Club. At the bar, I started talking to the leader of the band. He invited me to sit in and join them for a set on the small stage. After singing and playing a few songs, the manager came over and offered me a job playing weekends in the hotel. I was paid sixty-five dollars a month by the army and seventy-five dollars a night for playing and singing for a few hours at the hotel. It was clear to me which one was the better career choice.

While playing at the Bon Air I met a great, crazy songwriter named Jones Gilliland. Jones drove a car without a windshield. He wore sunglasses, even at night, so the bugs wouldn't get in his eyes while driving. His sometimes-girlfriend was also the friend of the general in charge of Fort Gordon. She sang at military luncheons, etc., and needed an accompanist. I got the job, which meant I was relieved of most of my other military duties, and spent the rest of my six months of active duty as her pianist.

I rented an apartment off base. At the end of the school year, Billi drove down in our Triumph to live with me for the summer.

Another interesting guy Billi and I met at the Bon Air was Dr. Jim. He was a young heart surgeon who took a liking to my music. One night we went to a party at his house and I remember two things: One was his bathtub, which was half filled with bathtub gin; The other was his kitchen, which was infested with local roaches called palmetto bugs. They were impossible to get rid of. Billi and I would sit on our patio and watch them fall out of the trees. Dr. Jim told me if I ever needed heart surgery, he would do it for free. After all these years, I sometimes wonder if his offer would still hold—if I ever needed his services.

When the summer ended, Billi returned to Reading to teach again. After a few months, I was discharged from active duty and returned to Billi and to playing at Stokesay.

All in all, my military career was relatively painless. I went to about a year of army reserve meetings and one summer training camp before joining a control group. In a control group you didn't have to go to meetings or summer camp because of your job. I worked weekends as a musician, which interfered with reserve meetings, so I was eligible. If your military occupation (MO) was needed anywhere in the country, you could be sent to active duty. My MO was radio signal engineer. It was a gamble, but I lucked out and was never called up, although I did get called to perform.

An officer in my unit, who helped me get into the control group, asked me to entertain the soldiers and their families at my last drill. Yes, I said. Then he asked if I ever performed outside of America. I once played a job in Canada, I replied. The officer had posters printed to announce my performance. He placed them around the reserve headquarters. The posters announced: INTERNATIONALLY KNOWN PAINIST BOBBY GOSCH WILL ENTERTAIN AT THE NEXT MEETING—BRING YOUR FAMILY. That misspelling of the word pianist was the army's parting shot in my short and weird military experience. After six years, I received an honorable discharge.

I did learn one lesson in the army. A friend of mine who had been in the service gave me a great piece of advice. He wisely said, "When you get called into formation for latrine duty or some other lousy job, always stand in the middle of the line. The guy in charge will always pick someone from one end or the other." My friend was correct.

Upon my return to normal civilian life, Billi and I moved into a larger, newly remodeled three-bedroom apartment in Reading, for $65 a month. I bought a 1919 American Cable grand piano, which I had rebuilt and refinished. It was well made and has the sound and touch I prefer. I still have it today.

5

ON TO NEW YORK

In 1962 Billi and I realized that Reading was a dead end for us. We decided to move to either Fort Lauderdale, Florida, or New York City. I thought there would be many opportunities for me to play in piano bars in both places. The plan was for Billi to secure a teaching job in the city of our choice, to provide us with an income while I got settled into the music scene. As it turned out, she secured job offers in both places. We chose New York City because it had the most possibilities for my musical career.

Now that I was pursuing a serious career in music, I became concerned that I was losing my hair in the front. I was not the type to even consider a hairpiece. Then I read an article in *Playboy* magazine about Jay Sebring, the top hairdresser in Hollywood. (He was later killed with Sharon Tate by Charles Manson's gang.) Sebring said the best look for a man losing his hair would be to shave it all off for a consistent, clean image. I took his advice. At the time it was a radical move. When I first shaved it all off, I would be walking the streets of New York and people would say, "Hey, there's Yul Brenner." A few years later it would be Mr. Clean and then Telly Sevalas. Today, a guy with a shaved head is as common as a guy who wears jeans. I also dropped the c in my last name, changing the spelling from Gosch to Gosh, so my name was easier to pronounce and remember. It also looked better in print for publicity.

While visiting with college friends who lived in Flushing, New York, we found a new one-bedroom apartment with an impressive marble bathroom for $125 a month just around the corner from them. You could see the future 1964 World's Fair grounds from the bedroom window. Billi passed the New York City Board of Education test and got a job teaching at Fresh Meadows Public School 26, which was nearby. We moved to Flushing in August 1962.

You had to be a member of Musician's Union Local 802 to play anywhere in New York City. The catch was that you had to live there for six months before you could join the union. The day after we moved, I went to meet a booking agent in Times Square. His office was a dingy, small room with only a desk and a small spinet piano. He was smoking a big cigar. The scene was right out of a Woody Allen movie. I played and sang three songs for him. As soon as I finished, he asked if I could work that night. I told him I didn't have a union card. He said, "Don't worry kid. The job is so far out on Long Island that a union agent will never show up there."

I started that night at a piano bar in Roslyn, Long Island. My pay was $125 for six hours a night and six days a week. The owner had rigged up a wire from the bar to the piano across the room and he would send musical requests down the wire. If someone requested the "Skater's Waltz," he would throw ice cubes at me. He was a nice guy with a good sense of humor, but I hated the job and the nights seemed to go on forever. To get there was a forty-five minute drive on the Long Island Expressway in my new Alfa Romeo Giulietta Spider. I was miserable, but it was a job and a paycheck and I was in New York.

After a few months of that, I was booked into a bowling alley underneath the elevated train tracks in Queens. Between the bowling pin strikes and the train noise, I doubt if anyone heard me play and sing. One customer said, "You're good, you should be playing in New York." I told him, "I thought I was in New York." Of course, he meant Manhattan, which was really my goal. I think I lasted one night playing in that place.

Next, I was booked into the Town House in Kew Gardens, Queens. The owner, Irv Gittelson, was also a very nice guy who loved music and ran a popular piano bar. Some of the waiters were aspiring to Broadway. I would accompany them as they sang Broadway standards during some of my sets. Irv was a lousy singer, but he loved to sing and I would have to accompany him whenever he got the urge, which was often.

The job had some nice perks—for one, I got to meet several great people. New York Yankees slugger Roger Maris lived across the street. He would always tuck into a corner banquette when he had a game in New York. Sometimes he would have a gorgeous, model-type young woman with him. He was a very shy, modest, nice guy, and was very friendly toward me. He gave me a signed photo of him connecting with the ball when he hit his famous sixty-first home run, breaking Babe Ruth's record. One night, the great tenor sax jazz player Stan Getz dropped by the bar on his way to the airport. I grabbed the opportunity to have a conversation with him. He was one of my jazz idols. I had watched him perform at Birdland when I was sixteen. And there I was, actually talking to him! Meeting people like Getz and Maris kept the job interesting.

The job turned out to have another great perk. Irv may have been a lousy singer, but he had a big heart. I told Irv that I would love to buy a new 1965 Ford Mustang, which had just been introduced but had a six-month waiting list. Irv motioned me over to the payphone as he made a call. He said into the phone, "Hello Lee, I need to get a new Mustang for a friend of mine." Irv asked me what color and accessories I wanted. He told Lee what I wanted and after he hung up, he told me an invoice would arrive in two weeks to pick up the car at a dealership in Westchester County, New York. The list price was $3,350, but I would pay $2,200, the dealer's price. Some dealers were charging inflated prices for the car because of the demand. The guy on the other end of the phone was, of course, Lee Iacocca, Irv's friend from college. Needless to say, I got a hell of a deal. Lee Iacocca conceived and developed the car, one of Ford's biggest successes. I drove the orange hardtop Mustang until 1968, when I traded it for a new Cadillac Eldorado.

After the Town House, I was booked into a jazz club on Long Island with a trio for two weeks. I had my union card, so I went to the union hall to find a drummer and a bass player. There I met Paul Motian and Teddy Kotick, who were both playing with Bill Evans, one of the all-time great influential jazz pianists. Evans was my absolute favorite jazz pianist. He would play beautiful lush chords, grabbing ten keys with ten fingers for one chord. His style was complex, refined and full of intellectual improvisation. He was a total original and many of today's jazz pianists have been influenced by him. Unfortunately, he was a heroin addict and known for not showing up for performances. I went to see him perform three different times in New York and San Francisco. He never showed up for any of them. He, of course, died many years ago. I had many of his albums that he did with Teddy and Paul. They were between gigs with Bill Evans and looking for temporary work. They agreed to play the two weeks with me for $25 a night each. I couldn't believe my luck. This made me realize that there was not a lot of money to be made playing jazz.

The job went well. They were incredible musicians, fun and inspirational to play with, but the customers were few and far between. The club owner loved jazz and had a beautiful room for performing. At the beginning of the second week, he told Paul and Teddy to take their instruments home and bring them back the next night. It was an unusual request, but the guys lugged their instruments home, as told.

The next morning, I received a phone call from the owner telling me, "The club burned to the ground last night after you left the job." Obviously, he knew he was going to burn the place, but respected musicians enough to not burn their valuable and cherished instruments. I never found out if he was arrested for arson. Teddy and Paul would have been interesting witnesses.

Next, my agent booked me to play the piano bar at the Forest Hills Inn in Queens. It was a well-known and popular place next to the famous tennis courts. Roger Williams was the pianist there, but he left because his recorded version of "Autumn Leaves" became a huge national hit. I enjoyed the job, which was about twenty minutes from our apartment. I stayed a few months. I remember a stock broker, who hung around the piano bar, trying to get me to buy some stocks from him when the Dow Jones was 600. His pitch was that the Dow was going to reach 1,000, but I didn't bite. I was working hard to earn my money and no way was I going to risk it on something I knew nothing about.

I might have lost my chance for millions, but I did make it big in New York. It just took one false start: My agent booked me into a restaurant on 44th Street off Times Square. I told all my friends in Pennsylvania that I finally made it. I was playing the big time in Manhattan. That night, waiting for me at the club, were flowers and telegrams of congratulations from friends. After the job, which I thought went well, I went up to the owner and said, "I'll see you tomorrow night."

He told me, "Oh no, this was just an audition."

I responded, "OK, I'll take my check."

He came back with, "Oh no, this wasn't a paid audition."

Extremely crushed, I complained to my booking agent to no avail and he booked me back into the Forest Hills Inn. After a few more months at the Inn, a customer there introduced me to Billy Reed, whose Little Club was one of the last great supper clubs in Manhattan, along with El Morocco. It was here that singer Doris Day debuted. You could get good food and good music. Billy's club was *the* hangout for show business celebrities.

Billy hired me as intermission pianist to play twenty-minute sets while the Latin music trio took its breaks. Billy didn't have a cabaret license allowing me to sing, but he let me sing anyway. The club was on 55th Street off Park Avenue and it was pure elegance—with deep, plush banquettes that ran along red velvet walls. It had a small, cozy bar up front, with the bandstand at the far end of the room. Billy, a short, bald guy in his late sixties, dressed stylishly in expensive suits, but had a bad habit of picking his nose at the bar when he thought no one was looking.

I was finally playing at a popular club in Manhattan and loved the job. Many celebrities came into the club. One night, as I was leaving for my forty-minute break, Barbra Streisand was waiting in the vestibule to get into the club, which was very crowded. She wasn't yet famous enough to avoid having to wait in line. One afternoon I played a private party for Hollywood star Joan Crawford at the club. She was quite friendly and consented to have a picture taken with me and Broadway singing stars Gordon and Sheila MacRae, who were at the party.

While at Billy Reed's, someone booked me on my off night to play a party at the 21 Club for the opening of *Camelot* on Broadway. Richard Burton was the star of the show. During the party, I repeatedly played and sang the entire *Camelot* musical score. At one point in the evening, Richard Burton and Elizabeth Taylor joined me on the piano bench, one on each side of me, as Richard sang the title song of the show.

No expense was spared for this grand affair. I remember a waiter with white gloves, who was parading around the room with a twenty-five-pound tin of Beluga caviar that he was liberally doling out to anyone who was interested. On my breaks I was interested and managed to snare my share.

During those early years in New York, I began making demo records of my songs so that I could promote them. The first recording studio I used in Manhattan in the mid-sixties was Associated Recording Studio. It was located in the same building as the Metropole, which was the bar I would visit on my trips to New York to hear the big bands when I was sixteen. I made demos there because the sound quality was good and it was inexpensive. The owners were nice guys and would be helpful in trying to make a project happen, especially for new talent. Many times when I recorded there, Paul Simon or another undiscovered star would be making song demos in one of the studios.

I met Jerry Samuels at Associated. He was a songwriter who at that moment had a big national comedy hit song on the radio. The song was "They're Coming to Take Me Away, Ha-Haaa!" and he recorded the song under the name Napoleon XIV. Samuels had no more songs for the follow-up album, so he asked me to write the songs. The follow-up album in those days could make you a lot more money and generate more hits.

I had previously met Jim Lehner, a comedy writer who wrote for the comedian Jonathan Winters. Jim was a short, sweet, funny guy, about five and a half feet tall. His wife was about six feet tall. Jim and I holed up in a room for two weeks and wrote all the songs. It took about a week to record them. The night we finished recording the album, we went to a bar to celebrate. We sat at the bar, deciding what we would do with all the money we were about to make. I think I chose buying a townhouse on the Upper West Side of Manhattan.

A few days later, a psychiatric association came out in the media stating the song was offensive and made fun of mental illness. Immediately, all radio play stopped; The album came out and sold nothing. Financially, I call the whole experience "a near miss." In later years I came to realize that the song was offensive to people with mental illness and I certainly would not take on such a project today. But at the time, writing the album seemed like a good idea, with an almost certain reward. At the least it was a great exercise in song writing.

6

SAMMY CAHN

One night at Billy Reed's Little Club, right before my last set, the place was almost empty except for one guy sitting alone at the bar. I recognized him as Sammy Cahn, the famous lyricist who wrote almost everything that Frank Sinatra sang. I mustered up the nerve to introduce myself and told him I had written some songs. He asked me to go to the piano and play and sing a few of my songs for him. When I finished I went back to the bar. Sammy told me he lived just around the corner at 55th Street and Lexington Avenue. He said, "If you are available at 11:00 A.M. tomorrow morning, come to my apartment and I'll fix your songs for you."

I couldn't believe my ears. I told Sammy, "I'll be there." I arrived on time the next morning and Sammy was very gracious. His apartment was small but immaculate. I later found out that he was building a very large marble house in Beverly Hills. Sammy asked me to go to the piano and play my best melody. I had a melody I really liked that had no lyric. I played it for Sammy and his only comment was, "Play it again."

I played it again and when I was finished he said, "Once more please." After I finished playing the song about three times, Sammy went over to his IBM Selectric typewriter and sat down. Sammy proceeded to type a lyric on the blank yellow paper. Things became very quiet for about a half hour, except for the clacking of his typewriter. Finally, Sammy got up, handed me the lyric, and said, "Sing this." I placed the yellow sheet of paper on the piano and proceeded to sing this new Sammy Cahn lyric to my melody. The title of the song became "The Need of You." I got chills and goose bumps as I sang and played the first line of the song for the first time: "I'm so lonely for the need of you, lonely only for the need of you." Together, those two words in the opening line, *lonely only*, created an internal rhyme. Sammy had put the stamp of his personal writing style on the song.

I finished singing the song and Sammy said, "I have to make a few adjustments, so play it again." I played the melody three or four more times while Sammy typed away on a new piece of paper. I sang the revised lyric and realized that this was a finished, good song. Then Sammy sang it through, while I played the piano to show me how to put inflections on certain words, much like Sinatra would.

The whole process took about an hour—I had just written a song with one of the best and most famous American lyricists! I left his apartment and felt like I was walking with my feet a foot off the ground.

Sammy traveled back and forth regularly from California to New York. Whenever he was in New York, he would call me and we would get together and write. At this time in his life, he was sort of between writing partners. Jimmy Van Heusen had been his last writing partner. Throughout his career, Sammy collaborated with many great composers, but in his later years he worked mainly with Van Heusen and Jule Styne. Sammy won four Academy Awards for his songs "All The Way," "Three Coins in the Fountain,"

"Call Me Irresponsible," and "High Hopes," and was nominated for twenty-two more.

He must have had more than one hundred bona fide hits among the hundreds of songs he wrote in his career. "Be My Love," "Come Fly With Me," "Day By Day," "Five Minutes More," "It's Been a Long, Long Time," "Love and Marriage," "Teach Me To-night," and "Let It Snow, Let It Snow, Let It Snow," to name just a few. You can see why I couldn't believe my good fortune that I was actually writing songs with him.

One day Sammy asked me to show up the next afternoon at Columbia Recording Studios on West 48th Street. Around 5:00 P.M., I walked into the studio and was ushered into the control room. As I opened the control room door, I heard a wonderful female voice singing "The Need Of You" with a very large orchestra. I looked around the control room and there was Sammy with a big smile on his face that seemed to say "Surprise!" The singer was Diahann Carroll and the fifty-three-piece orchestra was being conducted by Patrick Williams, who also arranged the music. The arrangement was gorgeous with a beautifully played violin solo in the introduction. As they ran through the song, I once again could not believe my ears. My song with lyrics by Sammy Cahn was being sung by a famous singer with a large orchestra. After the recording session, I went home and told Billi, "I am a real songwriter." It was one of the most exciting days of my life.

Sammy and I became very close friends. He was fifty-three years old and I was twenty-nine. Writing with Sammy was like getting my master's degree in songwriting. We wrote "Fun City" about New York, which got a lot of radio play in the city. We wrote special material for the comedian London Lee. Sammy was famous for writing special material for his friends, and I learned how to do that from him. He never took payment for that kind of work but would accept a gift. For the work with London Lee, I was given a beautiful down-filled club chair, which I still have today. I have sometimes written songs as my gift to close friends, to celebrate some special event, wedding, or birthday.

In 1965 Sammy began writing again with Jimmy Van Heusen. They wrote the score to two Broadway shows. First *Skyscraper* and then in 1966, *Walking Happy*. Sammy asked me to be a ghost writer to feed him lyric ideas when needed. He would call me from Philadelphia, or whatever town in which the show was running. The call would come around 11:00 P.M., after the show was over. He would say they needed a new song for a certain part of the show or they needed a new line for a certain song. I would then stay up all night trying to put new song lines and ideas together. Sammy would call me around 8:00 the next morning after getting a good night's sleep, and I would dictate my ideas and lines to him. He then spent the day writing new lyrics with some assistance from my lines and ideas, while I caught up on my sleep.

He used some of my lyrics and ideas in both shows. Billi and I were in the audience on the opening nights. It was a real kick to sit there and hear some of my words being sung on a Broadway stage. I was learning how to write for a Broadway show by sitting at the feet of a master lyricist. Sammy gave me a new state-of-the-art television set with remote control for my efforts.

Sammy had a great sense of humor. When I visited his new house in Beverly Hills, I noticed the license plates on the two cars in the driveway. Sammy's plate read "EARNS" and his wife Tita's plate read "SPENDS."

I was able to use my Broadway experience about a year later with Vaughn Meader, who had a very successful comedy record album called *The First Family*, a satire of President Kennedy and his family. It was the highest-selling record album of all time, until the Beatles came along. After Kennedy was assassinated, Vaughn's career took a nose dive. He later said, "The day President Kennedy died, I lost my life." Shortly after the nosedive, I played piano and organ on two of his comedy albums, and later we wrote a Broadway show *Simon Says*, which went nowhere. Vaughn died back in his home state of Maine in 2004.

While working with Vaughn, Sammy introduced me to Kenny Sheresky, a male model who owned a very attractive and popular steak house called Kenny's Steak Pub at 50th Street and Lexington Avenue. It was around the corner from the Waldorf Astoria Hotel. Kenny hired me to play piano and sing six nights a week in the bar room. I developed a good following of customers. In the beginning Kenny had told me the bar would wrap up around 11:00 P.M. After a few weeks, the crowd kept staying later because of the music. I ended up playing every night until 1:00 A.M.

Many customers were stockbrokers and stock tips were always being passed around. One waiter told me to buy McDonald's stock at eleven dollars per share, when it first came out. I asked, "What do they do?" He said, "They make and sell hamburgers." Not buying the pitch, I replied, "Just what we need, another hamburger stand." Big mistake! But I still won in the end. While playing at Kenny's, I became friends with a former Catskill comedian named Eddy Stern, who hung around the piano many nights. He was now a stockbroker and I trusted him. I gave him $8,000 to buy stock. By the end of the year it was worth $20,000. Definitely not a miss! I bought a new brown 1968 Cadillac Eldorado for $8,000 cash and traded in our 1965 Mustang.

I bought the Cadillac from a dealer in Pennsylvania, where my Dad had pumped gas for twenty-five cents an hour back in the early 1940s, when we lived on the farm. My parents went with Billi and me to pick up the new car. As we drove out of the dealership, my Dad, from the backseat, said, "I just don't believe this." He couldn't believe that his son just bought a new, expensive car for cash from the man he had worked for many years ago. When Dad died at the age of 63 in 1975, he was earning $15,000 a year as a machinist. This was enough to give his family a modest yet comfortable life.

A year later, the stock I bought from my friend Eddy Stern was worth only $8,000 again. I sold the stock and basically stayed out of the stock market forever. Another big mistake, but Wall Street can be a deadly game. Eddy said he was worth half a million dollars through trading, and he was planning to make it a million. Shortly thereafter, he had a heart attack. While in intensive care, he kept bugging the doctors and nurses for the day's copy of *The Wall Street Journal*. They finally relented and gave him a copy. The next day he died. I wanted to write a song about Eddy but never got around to it until a few years ago. I wrote "Killed by *The Wall Street Journal*" in memory of my friend Eddy Stern. The following song conveys my feelings about the greed that consumes Wall Street:

Killed by The Wall Street Journal

I'll tell you a story, every word of it true
It's a tale with a lesson, it'll be good for you
It's about getting everything you thought that you need
It's about getting rich, it's all about greed

It's all about Wall Street and my friend "Big Ed"
He started investing, gonna get rich he said
He talked about bankers and Goldman and Sachs
Read *The Wall Street Journal*, he could never relax
He entered a world a bit over his head
He never knew that he soon would be dead

He went long, he went short, he bought all kinds of ops
He hedged and he wedged, with his credit default swaps
I'm gonna be a player with the big guys he said
But he should've played the horses or gone to Vegas instead

He and the big boys were all on a roll
Then the moms and the pops jumped into the hole
Buy all that you can, it'll fly like a kite
Borrow tomorrow, there's no end in sight
Then one day they woke up and it all went bust
The hedges and wedges, there was no more trust

Big Ed read the news and grabbed hold of his chest
I'm ruined, I'm finished, it's over he confessed
They called 911 and the ambulance came
Took Ed to the IC and the end of the game

As he lay in his bed up in intensive care
He asked for *The Journal* for one last hope there
They brought the day's *Journal* to his hospital bed
"Dow drops one more thousand," the newspaper read
"My god, I'm wiped out," was all that Ed said
The monitor straight-lined and Big Ed was dead

He was killed by *The Wall Street Journal*
As sure as if shot by a gun
The hedges and wedges, they all did him in
And now it's all over and done.

While I am on the subject of Wall Street, I must tell one more story. In 1969, Sammy Cahn introduced Billi and me to his friend Ivan Boesky, a very interesting character. Sammy, the two of us, Ivan, and his wife Seema would sometimes meet socially. We would get together at the Beverly Hills Hotel in Hollywood or in Manhattan. Seema's family owned the Beverly Hills Hotel, which was just a few blocks from Sammy's house. Seema's father called Ivan: "Ivan the bum, with the hide of a rhinoceros and the nerve of a burglar."   Ivan was working on Wall Street. One summer day, Billi and I were in Central Park with our son Erik, who was one year old. We ran into Ivan, who was at the playground with his children. We sat on a bench together, talking while Erik was in a stroller and Ivan's kids played.

I clearly remember Ivan saying, "I think I'm going to buy a seat on the New York Stock Exchange."

By acting on those words, Ivan almost single-handedly destroyed Wall Street around 17 years later. In 1986, Ivan was indicted for insider trading in his arbitrage business. He made the cover of *Time* magazine, plea-bargained, aided the Feds in indicting some of his former colleagues, paid a fine of $100 million, and spent twenty-two months in jail. Ivan's manipulation of Wall Street was just another incident that soured me on investing in the stock market.

Also in 1969, Sammy Cahn introduced me to national TV exposure by way of "The Tonight Show." On the morning of Christmas Eve, Billi and I and our son Erik drove to

Pennsylvania to be with my parents for Christmas Eve. It was a three-hour drive from Manhattan. Before we left, Sammy asked for my parents' phone number and said he might have a surprise for me. I was at my parents' home for less than an hour when Sammy called and said, "Come back to New York immediately, you're going to be on television on 'The Tonight Show.'" I drove back to New York alone and walked into the NBC television studios around 5:00 P.M.

My Tonight Show performance happened because Sammy Cahn had brought the singer Jack Jones into Kenny's on occasion. Jack would sometimes sit on the piano bench with me and sing a song. Jack was Johnny Carson's guest host that night while Johnny took the night off. Jack's guests were Sammy, Steve Lawrence, Jayne Morgan, Paul Anka, and I. The producer, Fred DeCordova, decided that I would sing one song by myself and then all the others would gather around the piano and I would accompany them on the piano as each sang a song. I sang "Light My Fire" in my first exposure to a national television audience. The show was a success and I drove back to my family in Pennsylvania just in time to watch it at 11:30 P.M. (It had been taped earlier.) This was before videotape for consumers existed, so I took pictures of my performance directly off the TV screen. This was another one of the most exciting days of my life. I never get nervous while performing in concert, so performing for a national TV audience was a piece of cake. For months after that people would recognize me on the streets of New York and stop and talk about my appearance on "The Tonight Show."

It was time to start thinking about a manager. In 1967, while playing at Kenny's, I met Al Weissman, an assistant to Marty Erlichman, who managed Barbra Streisand (and still does). Al and Marty hung around the bar at Kenny's quite frequently. Al took an interest in me and talked about managing my career. I called him before I left Pennsylvania and told him about my appearance on "The Tonight Show." When I walked into the NBC studios, Al was already there talking to a lighting man at the piano saying, "Bobby likes the lights this way." On that day, Al officially became my manager.

Al was a balding, chubby, Jewish man of medium height in his mid-thirties. He believed in my talent. He was married, but also had a girlfriend, Sandy, who was nineteen years old. Al met Sandy the week she arrived in New York from Louisville, Kentucky. He managed her singing and acting career. Their affair lasted about ten years until Al's wife divorced him. Al then expected to marry Sandy, but she took up with another married man. Al remained her friend and manager until he died in 2008. During their affair, a friend of mine once asked me if Al was "still eating two Thanksgiving dinners?" which I thought was hilarious. Sandy died in 2013.

A few years after Al started managing me, Marty Erlichman began to manage a famous country singer. Marty sent Al on the road to oversee him while he performed at country and western dance halls and road houses. Al had two main duties. One was to carry a gun and collect the singer's payment in cash from the ticket sales during the performance intermission. If he wasn't paid in full for his show, the singer wouldn't perform the second half. That's how some of the country music circuits worked in those days.

After the show, Al's other duty was to supervise and line up all the women waiting at the star's hotel room door to have sex with him. He must have been one hell of a stud. Womanizing was an occupational hazard then for male entertainers, same as today. But it was one I never took up.

Al secured many record company contracts for me over the years: Polydor, ABC Paramount, RCA, and Capitol Records. In 1967 Marty Erlichman had invited me and my trio to be the warm-up act for Barbra Streisand's legendary CBS television performance, "A Happening in Central Park." The audience of 240,000 people was the largest crowd any performer had drawn to a Central Park concert. I did not appear on the televised show, but it still was an unbelievable experience. I can still picture Barbra coming onto the stage, built over a large rock, in her billowing, white, diaphanous chiffon gown. I was certainly experienced in performing for large crowds after Barbra's concert.

Soon after, Marty came into Kenny's and said, "Pack your bags, you're going to California to become Barbra's conductor, pianist, and musical director." I thought, *This is incredible. I am going to be Barbra Streisand's musical director.* The next morning Marty called me and said Barbra had chosen someone else. What a near miss! But there was always tomorrow, with another opportunity.

7

PAUL ANKA

While playing at Kenny's Steak Pub, Sammy Cahn introduced me to Paul Anka. In 1967 Billi and I moved from Queens to Manhattan. Our apartment was at 333 East 79th Street on the 21st floor. It was a one- and-a-half bedroom with two full baths and a spectacular view of Manhattan facing downtown. Paul lived nearby at 86th and Park Avenue. A few nights a week, when I finished performing around 1:00 A.M., he would call me at Kenny's and ask if I wanted to write songs. Paul was an insomniac. I would go up to his apartment and we would write songs until 4:00 or 5:00 A.M.

Early one morning we were writing while the TV was on in the background. I don't remember what was going on, but it was very bad news. It seemed like the Third World War was imminent. Paul looked at me with a very serious stare and said, "The fucking world is coming to an end and here we are, trying to write a fucking song."

Almost immediately, Paul asked me to be his pianist whenever he went on tour. Of course I accepted. After about six months, he asked me to be the conductor of his thirty-two piece orchestra. I knew the orchestral arrangements from playing the piano in his shows, but I had never actually conducted an orchestra. I accepted his offer, but began to panic immediately when I realized the responsibility I had accepted.

Back in 1963, I studied orchestration for a year at Juilliard School of Music in Manhattan with Jacob Druckman, a Pulitzer Prize-winning composer. Each week we would learn how to write for a different section of the orchestra. On Mondays we learned the ranges and other intricacies of the instrument. If it was a string section that week, we would write an arrangement for that section. On Friday we would go to class and there would be a group of student string players to play our arrangements. It was an unbelievable and stimulating experience and was extremely useful for the rest of my career.

So I called Juilliard and asked them for the name of a good conducting teacher. I called the teacher and he said, "I charge $100 an hour." I asked him if he could give me a three-hour lesson the next day because I had to conduct a thirty-two-piece orchestra at Grossinger's in the Catskills that coming Saturday night. I showed up at his apartment on Park Avenue. I was greeted by a distinguished-looking Italian gentleman, about sixty years old, dressed in a beautiful, burgundy, velvet smoking jacket. The living room was about sixty feet long. At the far end was a full-size concert grand piano. He instructed me to sit at the piano, as I would be conducting from the piano, and proceeded to show me how to give forceful downbeats, which is the first beat of the song, and explained other general conducting techniques. In three hours he taught me how to be in full charge of the orchestra.

It was the best three hundred dollars I ever spent and I went on to successfully conduct my first show on Saturday night. I was fortunate to have one of best show drummers in the country, Sol Gubin, as Paul's drummer. All I had to do was throw the downbeat and Sol would set the tempo from there. Then I would just follow Sol's beat.

Setting the pace of the beat of the song is the most crucial part of backing up a singer. It must be just right for the singer, not too fast and not too slow. Sol's timing was impeccable, so as a beginning conductor I was fortunate to have him make this important decision for me.

A conductor for a pop singer is basically a green light traffic cop. The conductor must rehearse the orchestra. After that, the well-rehearsed musicians could play the show without a conductor, except for one thing: Conductors tell musicians the exact moment to start playing and establish the tempo or speed of the song. That is all the conductor is needed for. The rest of the motions are basically just for show.

A classical music symphony conductor must be a kind of genius. He (or she) is also a traffic cop, but he is standing in the middle of the busiest traffic circle in Rome. He is calling all the shots for all the cars going every which way. The rehearsed expert musicians could play without the conductor, if someone starts them. But the conductor interprets the volume of the music for the players, which constantly changes each time a soloist or section enters into the music. The conductor interprets his vision of how the music should be played to the musicians in real time. Also, the tempos of a symphonic score change constantly as the music proceeds, so a conductor is absolutely necessary. The conductor's responsibility is to accurately convey what the composer intended when he wrote the music.

Sol was a freelance drummer and studio musician who backed up Frank Sinatra, Peggy Lee, and many other great singers. He was a legend among New York musicians and the funniest man I ever met. He looked like Bill Maher, but with a large, hooked nose and Groucho Marx glasses. Musically, I was out of his league, but we became close friends and he helped me become a serviceable conductor. Sol could play a show without a rehearsal if necessary because he was an excellent sight reader. It was said about him that if a fly crapped on a music page, he would read the fly spec and play the note.

Sol was married, but also was a ladies' man. I did not play that game. We flew all over the world together with Paul. Within ten minutes on an airplane, he would have all the stewardesses laughing with him and giving us extra drinks and food. During long international flights in the late quiet hours of the night, he was also a member of the "Mile High Club." Sol loved to get high on cocaine and marijuana.

One night he was trying to talk a woman he just met into smoking some marijuana. She said, "But isn't it habit forming?"

Sol's answer was, "Hell no, and I should know. I've been doing it for twenty-five years."

Another story, which I heard and Sol verified, was that he drove to Las Vegas in his brand new Porsche to play drums for Peggy Lee. He gambled heavily while there and lost. He had to leave the Porsche with his creditors in Vegas and go home on the bus.

When Paul performed in Puerto Rico, we would hang around the swimming pool and get a little high at the El San Juan Hotel during the day. Suddenly the loudspeaker would bark: "Telephone call for "Miss Connie Lingus," or "Telephone call for Manuel Labor." Of course, it would be Sol requesting the phone pages with the best Spanish accent he could muster. At the bar he would always order a Penis Colossus.

I experienced my first really incredible marijuana hallucination with Sol. It taught me the dangers of not knowing the strength of the marijuana you are consuming. We were playing with Paul at the Fontainebleau Hotel in Miami Beach. We arrived by plane to Miami and had an immediate late afternoon rehearsal to prepare for the evening performance. Sol and I returned to our rooms, which were in a row of cabanas right beside the ocean. I had three puffs from a small pipe full of what Sol said was "great grass."

We agreed to meet for dinner as soon as we got dressed in our tuxedos for the show. I walked into my room and closed the door. When Sol arrived to pick me up after he got dressed, I was still hanging on the doorknob inside the door. He had smoked more than me, appeared to be totally normal, and was having a big laugh at my condition. He told me to meet him at the bar after I dressed, and left me alone.

I took off my clothes and noticed that the clock said seven sharp. I went into the bathroom to brush my teeth. Upon looking down into the sink bowl, I had the feeling that I was crawling into the drain. After brushing my teeth, I looked again at the clock. It still said exactly seven sharp and did not appear to have moved even a second.

Then I noticed a few dead palmetto bugs in certain corners of the room. These are roach-like creatures about one to two inches long that are very common in Florida. (Billi and I had encountered them in Georgia too.) I became aware of the powerful sound of the ocean. I felt I had absolutely no control over my mind. For an instant, I thought that for whatever reason Sol had drugged me and I was going insane. My feelings fluctuated between insanity and the possibility that I may already be dead or in the process of dying. I would "reason" that I really was going insane and was destined to spend the rest of my life in this helpless limbo. Then I kept telling myself that I could figure out what was happening to me and there must be a logical answer to my condition, other than insanity. So, my mind wandered back to the theory that I must in fact be dying. I heard the ocean again and knew that I now had the answer. I "reasoned" that a Russian submarine must be out there somewhere in the ocean and was dispensing some sort of chemical warfare on the Florida coast. I was in the process of dying from this chemical and the lower forms of life, namely the palmetto bugs, were already dead. I was obviously hallucinating and having a paranoid episode.

I was also helpless to remove myself from the room to look for other possible survivors. I lay down on my bed with the side of my head on the pillow and watched my lower lip flow all over the bed like a Salvador Dali soft watch. And then I fell asleep.

About 9:00 P.M., I was awakened by Sol knocking on the door. I was still quite shaken, but able to function normally. Sol thought my story was hilarious. He had been drinking at the bar and noticed that it was almost show time and I had not yet appeared, so he came looking for me. He assured me that he had consumed more grass than me, and he had done nothing to cause my condition. I believed him. I went on to perform a successful show.

This account is accurate because I wrote it down the day after the incident in 1968, intending to write a book about marijuana. I kept the notes all these years. Looking back, it now sounds like the incident came right out of Hunter Thompson's book *Fear And Loathing In Las Vegas* and the movie of the same name starring Johnny Depp. I experienced a classic paranoid, hallucinogenic event from smoking too much potent marijuana. This event warned me to never cross the line into hallucination, but I never regretted having done it that one time.

What I learned from that experience and other later experiences was that different people can react in extremely different ways to an identical amount of the same batch of marijuana. Sol was more experienced than I and had a greater tolerance than I did for consuming an even larger amount of the same grass. The body seems to build a tolerance to marijuana, as the user builds up his personal file of experiences. It also occurs to me that after a period of abstinence, one could have a stronger response to a given potency of the drug. I'll say more about all of this in a later chapter. After this, I approached marijuana much more cautiously.

I conducted the thirty-two-piece orchestra for Paul whenever he booked a date or tour. Sometimes it would be a week or two at the Copacabana night club in Manhattan. We would play Las Vegas anywhere from one week to a month at a time. I was in Vegas about five times with Paul, playing the Sands, Flamingo, and other hotels. Billi was with me on one of the month-long trips to Vegas, along with our nine-month-old son, Erik. One day we were sitting by the deep end of the pool with Erik between us. We heard a car accident happen in the street. Billi and I turned around to look at it for about ten seconds. When we turned back, Erik was laying at the bottom of the pool. Fortunately, Billi had been a life guard during high school and college. She dove in and retrieved Erik immediately. He spit out some water and Billi took him back to the shallow end of the pool. He began laughing and paddling in the water, as if nothing had happened.

We played the biggest night club in Mexico City a few times. On the first day, when we got to the club for a rehearsal, we were greeted by a couple of guys trying to sell the band members cocaine and marijuana. I was told that the pushers were members of the Federales, the national police. It was said that they were trying to sell us the drugs they had confiscated from the Mexican pushers they arrested. That's the way it worked in Mexico, and it probably still does. They did make some sales to Sol, as I remember.

Whenever Paul performed outside of New York City, we traveled with eight musicians and picked up the rest of the orchestra at the venue where we were playing. We travelled with the rhythm section: Sol, a guitar player, a bass player, and I. We also brought along a lead trumpet player, a lead saxophonist, a lead trombonist, and the great Cuban bongo player Chino Pozo. When available, the bass player was Milt Hinton. Milt is a legend to all musicians. He worked with everyone from Charlie Parker to Louis Armstrong to Frank Sinatra and many others in hundreds of performances and recording sessions. Milt was a master bass player and a great photographer, who took pictures of all the star musicians he performed with over all the years. His photos were published in a book titled *Bass Line* in 1988. He died on December 19, 2000, at the age of 90. His obituary took up a half page in *The New York Times*. His nickname was "The Judge." Milt was a mentor to me, and I was very fortunate to be in his company. As Quincy Jones said in Milt's book, "Milt Hinton is one of those rare people who has seen and lived most of the history of jazz."

The only guy we traveled with who did not get high or do drugs was Chino the bongo player. He was of small and thin stature, had a mustache and slicked-back black hair. He practiced Voodoo and always wore a red suit, red hat, and red stockings for good luck when he was flying in airplanes. He made an authentic Cuban dish of rice with chicken (*arroz con pollo*) if it was requested of him.

Even though he never did any drugs, Chino would always be taken to a room in every airport and strip searched. One time, they held him for almost an hour and even looked up his ass in disbelief that he wasn't carrying drugs.

We toured Sweden and played twenty different cities in one month. When we were leaving the Stockholm airport to return to a gig in Las Vegas, they bumped us from the flight even though we all had confirmed tickets. We had a five-hour delay until the next flight. Some of the guys bought bottles of Aquavit at the duty free shop and proceeded to get completely drunk. The lead trumpet player was so wasted that he found a scooter somewhere and rode it straight through a large plate glass window, cutting his arms. He got medical attention and somehow we all made the next flight back to the United States.

Because we were bumped from the flight, we missed our connection in New York and were late for the rehearsal in Vegas the next day. Paul's lawyer sued the airline for the missed rehearsal. The airline settled by giving Paul $10,000 plus $500 to each musician.

In late September of 1968, I traveled with Paul to a music festival in Rio De Janiero, Brazil. We had been there a week when I got a call in the middle of the night from a friend who said he just took Billi, who was pregnant, to the hospital. I left Brazil immediately after receiving the call, but still missed our son Erik's birth. He was born the next day, two weeks early, on October 5.

One thing I will always remember about the Rio trip, was going with Paul to a party at a private residence and seeing the king of all Bossa Nova composers, Anton Carlos Jobim, sitting on a sofa with his guitar and singing his hit songs. Paul and I were hanging out a lot in Rio with Dinah Shore, a very popular singer at the time who was also there for the music festival. Dinah was sitting on the couch with Jobim and sang a few songs with him. Hearing Jobim perform in such an intimate setting remains as one of my most special musical memories.

I made $750 a week when I traveled with Paul and $250 a week on retainer when we weren't working. When we didn't work, I continued performing at Kenny's Steak Pub to supplement my income. Paul and I continued to write songs together during this whole period. Paul got some of the songs we wrote recorded by Tommy James and the Shondells, Englebert Humperdinck, country singer Ray Price, Trini Lopez, and others. "We Made It Happen," which we wrote together, was recorded by Englebert Humperdinck. It was the title song of the album and a half million copies were pressed without my name on the record as co-writer. Paul apologized and said it was a mistake. I did have songwriter contracts on all the songs we wrote together and I did receive royalties, but I needed the credit on the records to further my songwriting career. After my objection on the omission, later CD versions of the album did give me credit.

The Tommy James song we wrote together, "Run Away with Me," was on the *Mony Mony* album on Roulette Records. The album was a big hit. Paul and I were due royalties because we were on the hit album. I asked Paul why we weren't getting any royalties for the song and Paul said something like "That's Morris, and he's known for not paying royalties." Morris Levy, the head of Roulette Records, was said to be connected to the mob, so no one ever seemed to question him about royalties that were owed.

Paul and I wrote a song called "853 Tenth Avenue" that was also released on Roulette. It was my first national release of a recording with me as the singer. The song went nowhere, though it recently has turned up on the internet as a good, but ignored record. Even if the song had become a hit, I'm sure Morris would not have paid me any royalties. The word on the street seemed to be *Don't talk to Morris about royalties, unless you want your knees broken*. He was a colorful figure in the music business, to say the least.

When we wrote together, Paul would repeatedly suggest that we write an English lyric to a hit French song "Comme d'Habitude," for which he had the American publishing rights. I told him I was not interested and preferred to write new original songs. Another big mistake. I could not have imagined the hit it would become.

One night when we were playing at the Flamingo Hotel in Las Vegas, I went to Paul's suite before the show to get the order of songs for that night's performance. There on the piano were the lyrics Paul wrote for the French melody. Paul couldn't play much piano, so he asked me to play and sing his new song. I knew the melody well because of all the times he talked about the song. I sat down at the piano... "And now, the end is near, and so I face the final curtain." I finished the song, looked at Paul, and said, "That sounds like a hit." The song was "My Way."

After they both finished their shows, Paul was playing baccarat every night with Sinatra, who was also in Vegas performing. Paul said he was going to present "My Way" to Sinatra, for whom he wrote the lyric. He was very excited and told me to meet him the next morning at United Recording Studios in Vegas, where we would make a piano and voice demo of the song for Sinatra. The next morning I was in the studio waiting for Paul, when he called and said he had laryngitis. The doctor said if he sang the demo, he wouldn't be able to sing the show that night. He told me to make the demo by myself.

I proceeded to sing and play the song, pretending I was Sinatra so the engineer in the control room could get a balance and proper sound levels. At the end of the first run-through, the engineer pushed the talk back button, and said, "What the fuck was that?" I said, "It's Paul Anka's new song, 'My Way,' which he wrote for Frank Sinatra." The engineer said, "That's a fucking hit song." It was that obvious.

The engineer cut three acetates: one for Sinatra, one for Paul, and one for me. (Unfortunately, I lost my copy of the demo when I moved from Manhattan to Vermont in 1975. The demo would certainly have been a part of the song's musical history and I wish I still had it.) I took two demos over to Paul's suite. Acetates preceded tapes and cassettes and were cut individually onto a lacquer-coated disc to store the music. Paul played the demo and was happy with it. He said he was sending it over to Frank Sinatra's suite at his Vegas hotel. Frank was waiting to hear it.

Before the show that evening, I went over to Paul's suite. He had a big smile on his face and asked how much money I lost gambling. I told him I didn't gamble. He handed me five one-hundred-dollar bills for making the demo. He said Sinatra was going to record "My Way" the following Monday in Hollywood with a fifty-piece orchestra. The music was arranged and conducted by Don Costa. Two weeks later "My Way" was climbing the charts and the rest is musical history. It became Sinatra's signature song and went on to be recorded by hundreds of singers from the Sex Pistols to Pavarotti. The song has made millions of dollars for Paul and the two writers of the original French melody, all of whom share in the royalties. It was a songwriter's dream come true.

When a singer records an already established hit song, it's called a cover record. When many other singers cover a hit song, it becomes an even bigger hit. All the cover records, usually on albums, generate more income for the songwriter. The song becomes even more famous due to all the additional exposure. Thus, it is a songwriter's dream come true.

Soon after "My Way" became a hit, I traveled with Paul to London, where he performed with a famous singer. The singer shall remain nameless for obvious reasons. One night we were driving in a Rolls Royce on the M1 highway. Paul and I were in the back seat with the singer's young girlfriend between us. Paul asked the singer to come up to our suite at the Dorchester hotel so that we could play a new song we wrote for him. It was the same spacious suite used by Richard Burton and Elizabeth Taylor when they were in London. The suite had two bedrooms with a large living room between them. Paul had the hotel put a small spinet piano in the living room so that we could write songs. As soon as we walked in, the singer disappeared into a bedroom with the girl. A little later he called from the bedroom for us to call the desk for a taxicab for the girl. The girl came out, said goodbye, and left. The singer then came out of the bedroom balls-ass naked and said, "Play me the song." He leaned on the piano as I played and Paul sang the song "My Double Life," about a guy who is cheating on his wife. I sat at the piano at eye level with the singer's limp junk, while Paul sang. This had to be one of the weirdest song pitches of all time. We finished the song and the singer said he liked it. He never recorded it. Buddy Greco, a popular jazz singer at the time, recorded it and I recorded it on my first Polydor album.

On yet another night in London, another strange thing happened. Paul and I went to a party at a townhouse. When we got there, a stripper, at least sixty years old, was dancing naked in the living room, while a white chinchilla crawled all over her body. While this was happening, I noticed some people going upstairs. I followed them into a room with a one-way mirror. A bunch of people were watching what was happening on the other side of the mirror. Three men and four women were naked in a huge bed, participating in a lively sex orgy. The owner of the townhouse sure knew how to throw a party.

Nevertheless, despite the good money, the talented musicians I got to work with, and the amusing-if-strange experiences I had, working with Paul was getting to be more and more difficult. Paul secured a recording of one of our songs, "Easy To Say," with a popular vocal group the Vogues. Months later when we were in Las Vegas, I went to Paul's suite and noticed a record on his desk. It was the Vogues record, which had just been released, and my name was not credited as co-writer. The writers credited were Paul Anka and the manager of the Vogues, who had made no contribution to the song except to get it recorded. This was part of my education about how the music business worked, and still does.

In March, 2015, the Marvin Gaye estate won a plagiarism law suit against the writers of Robin Thicke's 2013 huge hit song "Blurred Lines." The credited writers were Thicke, the rapper T.I., and Pharrell Williams. During the trial, Thicke admitted he didn't write a note or word of the song, but demanded credit anyway because he was the singer. He said, "The biggest hit of my career was written by somebody else and I was jealous and wanted credit." The Gaye estate won a $5.7 million settlement.

For me, the Vogues record was the final straw. We were supposed to leave Las Vegas in two weeks for a tour of Australia. I was getting tired of being on the road and missing Billi and our new son Erik. I was so upset with Paul for not giving me credit on the record that I gave him my two weeks' notice on the spot and said I would not be going to Australia with him. That night, at the end of the show, he did not introduce me on stage as his conductor, nor did he for the remainder of the Vegas shows. He also told me that he would see to it that I never would work in the music business again. That was the dark side of Paul.

I wasn't the only person to have borne the brunt of it either. There was a bar on 48th Street in Manhattan called Jim and Andy's, where all the musicians hung out—including a bunch of Paul's former conductors and musicians. They joked about being members of "The Ex-Paul Anka Conductor's and Musician's Club." I became an official member.

Years later, when Michael Jackson died, they released the video of his last rehearsals for the show he never did. The video was called "This Is It," after the title of one of the songs in the show. Michael Jackson got sole credit for the song. Paul came out in the news media and said he wrote the song with Michael in 1983. Eventually the estate of Jackson admitted that Paul did indeed write the song with Michael. Ironically, Paul got a small temporary dose of what it feels like to not get credit for something he helped write—although he eventually got writer's credit and made a lot of money on the Michael Jackson video and CD sales.

Even though I had some problems with Paul regarding the songwriting credits, working with him proved to be a major move in my music career.

8

JIMMY WESTON'S

Back in the Billy Reed's Little Club days I would spend my forty-minute intermission breaks at a little bar around the corner called The Camel Driver. The first night I walked in, dressed in my tuxedo, the owner, Jimmy Weston, came over and introduced himself. I told him I played and sang at Billy Reed's. Jimmy told the bartender that my drinks would always be half price. That sealed the deal. It became my hang-out place during my intermissions. I also ate there because the food was good.

Jimmy was an ex-narcotics detective on the New York police force and a charismatic guy. The subject of my marijuana use never came up in our relationship. He was a good-looking Irishman with a bent nose, probably from an altercation in his police work. He had a winning personality and was an excellent promoter of his establishment. One Friday night he came over to me, looking a little upset. He needed $1,000 to carry some obligations over the weekend, until he could cash in his American Express charges the following Monday.

One of my rules has always been to never lend money to friends because that is a bank's job. But I trusted Jimmy and had a good gut feeling. I wrote him a check. When I walked into his bar the following Monday night, Jimmy handed me $1,000 cash. From then on we became very good friends.

Toward the end of my Paul Anka years, I would still play at Kenny's Steak Pub when I was in town. Jimmy came over one night and asked me to go with him on my break to see something. We walked a few blocks to a vacant restaurant on 54th Street between Park and Lexington avenues. The closed steak house had been called Chateaubriand in its better days and was well known. It was a comfortable space in a great location. It was at least four times larger than Jimmy's place.

Jimmy said, "If you say you'll perform here, I'll move my restaurant here and make this a fine dining spot with continuous music like the Hickory House." The Hickory House was where Billy Taylor, Marian McPartland, and other famous jazz pianists performed. I used to go there when I was in high school to hear Billy Taylor play. On the spot I agreed. Jimmy said, "Go to Steinway on 57th Street and pick out any piano you want and I'll buy it." This opportunity was unheard of in my experience. I said I would also need an Echoplex echo chamber, which had just come on the market, and a great sound system. Jimmy said, "Knock yourself out." He also planned to hire an intermission pianist and singer to keep the music going nonstop when my trio was on a break. I gave my notice at Kenny's Steak Pub.

I went to Steinway and tried out about ten pianos. Each piano has its own personality. The sound of the piano is of utmost importance. The touch or feel of how the mechanical action responds when your fingers hit the keys is also extremely important. Every pianist has his or her own preference. For Jimmy's new restaurant, I chose a five-foot-seven-inch grand piano (to fit on the small stage) with the bright sound and light keyboard touch I prefer.

Once again, my gut feeling about Jimmy proved to be worth following. He opened his new club, Jimmy Weston's, a few months later. He knew everybody in the nightclub business and the place was an immediate success. There was a uniformed door man and a maître d' in a tuxedo named Nick, who also knew many people. If someone coming from the airport asked a cab driver where the action in town was, he would tell them Jimmy Weston's. After you walked through the front vestibule, you entered a large room with a long bar along the left wall. It was always packed with sports stars and celebrities. If you wished to eat or be close to the music, Nick would greet you and usher you to a banquette in the plush back dining room. At the far end of the room was a small raised stage where I performed. The food was excellent, and my musicians and I ate for free, which was a great perk. I hired the best sidemen in the city. Don Payne, a top studio musician, became my bass player. Denny Seiwell, who had just arrived in New York, became my drummer. Later on Paul McCartney hired Denny to play in his new band, Wings. I wished him well and hired Alan Schwartzberg, another top studio musician. Alan later left my trio to join the band on "The David Letterman Show."

Jimmy was very flexible. When I went out on tour with Paul Anka, the intermission pianist would take over my spot, or Jimmy would hire a well-known pianist like Barbara Carroll or Marian McPartland. Whenever I was in town, it was my job. After I left Paul, I played fulltime at Jimmy Weston's. I was performing mostly my own songs and played three shows a night. When we performed, everybody in the room listened.

My breakup with Paul was the right decision. Things were going well. I was also starting to write and produce music for radio and television commercials at a little recording studio called Twelve East. The owner, George, was a nice guy and taught me a lot about making commercials. I was earning $750 a week playing at Jimmy's and an average of $750 for each commercial I wrote, plus the Screen Actor's Guild fees and residuals for singing them, which is where the real money was. All in all, it was very good money at the time.

The sports stars and celebrities who came into Weston's, drew the general public. The star Russian ballet dancer Rudolph Nureyev would come in whenever he was in town. He stayed with the actress Mamie Van Doren and they would come in together.

In 1971, my manager, Al Weissman, brought in the artist and repertoire—or A&R—man Jon Sagen from Polydor Records to hear me perform. The A&R man's job is to find performers, sign them to a contract, and produce the recordings. Jon was impressed and offered me a two-album deal, with a $50,000 budget for each album. At the time that was the standard good deal for a recording contract with a big name label. It cost about $5,000 per song to hire top musicians and record in the best recording studios.

I wanted to write a song for the album for my son Erik, who was now three years old. One evening Billi and I went to dinner in New Jersey at the home of my old stock broker friend, Eddy Stern. On the coffee table was a small booklet with Rudyard Kipling's poem "If." I read it and said to myself, *This is what I want to say to my son.* Eddy gave me the poem. The next day, back at our apartment in Manhattan, I wrote a melody for the poem. I called the song "A Song for Erik (Rudyard Kipling's Poem 'If')." I wanted to record the song for my first Polydor album, but immediately realized the poem was written in 1936, the same year I was born, and was still under copyright. This meant I couldn't adapt the poem to my music without permission of the copyright owner.

A few nights later I played the song in my show at Jimmy Weston's. After I finished singing, a guy came up to the stage with tears in his eyes. He introduced himself as Nelson Doubleday, the CEO of the publishing company Doubleday that published all of Kipling's works in America. What a coincidence! Some people might call this the Hand of God, but as a budding atheist, I call it being at the right place at the right time. Nelson told me that Kipling was his godfather. When he was a little boy, Kipling gave him a postage stamp on the back of which Kipling had written the entire poem "If," using a magnifying glass. Kipling only did this twice in his lifetime.

I said to Nelson, "I have a problem. I want to record the song, but need permission to use the poem." The very next day he had secured permission for me to use the poem from the National Trust of Great Britain, which controlled the copyright. Nelson said I would receive the formal legal papers in a few weeks, which I did. The only other time the trust gave permission to use a Kipling poem for a song was for Frank Sinatra to record "On the Road to Mandelay." I recorded "If" and finished my first Polydor album, titled *Bobby Gosh,* in 1971. Nelson died in June, 2015.

The musicians and I consumed large amounts of marijuana during the recording sessions. The album was released nationally to some positive critical acclaim. The review in *Playboy* magazine noted: "Despite all the tricky redundancy and careful mimicry in so much pop music, individual voices and styles do appear that project the kind of integrity you hear in *Bobby Gosh* (Polydor). The music in these grooves sounds like a very personal composite of Richie Havens, Elton John, and James Taylor, with a rough but winning voice." The review also noted that the "backings are beautifully done, and the album does sustain the promise of the opening track, 'As Long As She Will Stay.'" For me, this confirmed that my time studying orchestration at Julliard was well worth it.

9

SINATRA

One night at Jimmy Weston's, after my breakup with Paul, Frank Sinatra walked in. The place was buzzing with excitement because he was in the room. He seemed to be enjoying himself and the customers didn't bother him. They were used to celebrities being in attendance. When I came to work a few nights later Nick, the maître d', told me, "Frank is here with Tony Bennett and a party of ten, right in front of the stage. He said he came with some friends to hear you perform."

I climbed onto the stage and saw Frank's party directly in front of me, seated at a long table with Frank facing me at the far end. I played the introduction to the first song and saw Frank hush the table with his two hands. For my entire forty-five-minute set, the group was totally attentive and quiet, except for applause at the end of each song. I could hardly believe I was really performing for Frank Sinatra and Tony Bennett, two of my singing idols. It was very heady and flattering to have Sinatra care about listening to me perform. I will never forget it. Tony Bennett's first hit, "Cold, Cold Heart," was one of the first popular songs I learned to play professionally, twenty-one years earlier when I was fourteen years old.

Shortly after my first Polydor album was released, Frank was in Weston's again and I gave him a copy. A few weeks later, as I walked past the booth he always sat in, a hand reached out and grabbed mine, pulling me into the booth. It was Frank. "I'd like you to meet my friend, Ava Gardner," he said. She was beautiful and charming. For the first time, I was actually sitting and talking with Frank Sinatra!

He kept me at his table for my entire forty-five-minute break. His charisma was powerful. The whole time, I had his and Ava's complete attention. He made you believe you were the only person in the room. At the end of the conversation, he said he was going to record "A Song for Erik" (Rudyard Kipling's Poem 'If')" from my album.

I went home and told Billi, "I finally made it! Frank Sinatra is going to record 'If.'" About a month later, Frank announced his first retirement and never recorded the song. Another near miss—and not the first with Sinatra: Back when I was writing with Paul, we wrote a song called "Next Year." Paul got Frank to agree to record it. It was the fifth song on the music stand at a Sinatra recording session. Frank started to lose his voice after the fourth song and he never recorded "Next Year." Paul recorded it a little later.

It may have been another near miss with Frank, but "If" was later recorded by Roger Whitaker, Mike Douglass, Sandler and Young, and John Davidson. Not quite a substitute for Frank.

10

TOURING AND CAROL HALL

My manager, Al Weissman, got me signed with the William Morris Agency. In 1971, the agency booked me on various dates around the country to promote my Polydor album. I played colleges as the opening act for Three Dog Night and Sha Na Na. When I opened for Three Dog Night in front of 20,000 people, I used their sound system. I did not do a sound check and when I struck the first notes of my first song, the piano sounded like a canon going off. It was so loud that I thought the roof was going to cave in. Fortunately, my voice was mixed just as loudly. This was my first experience with state-of-the-art rock and roll stadium sound. The Streisand concert in Central Park was over ten times the crowd and the sound system covered about three city blocks, but the Three Dog Night concert was indoors, so all the sound was contained in one huge space.

William Morris also booked me into a night club in San Francisco called the Boarding House. I was the opening act for the great jazz singer Morgana King. (She later played the mother in the Godfather movies.) Morgana recorded "As Long As She Will Stay" from my album for her album *New Beginnings*, and she was singing the song in her act. Because our rooms were in the same hotel, I got to watch a then-young, unknown photographer named Annie Liebowitz photograph Morgana for an article in *Rolling Stone*.

On opening night at the Boarding House, I walked into my dressing room and was greeted by a bottle of Beaulieu Vineyards 1968 private reserve wine. It was a gift from the Polydor Records promoter who was in charge of taking care of me and promoting my album at the local radio stations. Until that time, the only wines I ever tasted were Liebfraumilch and Mateus, two rather mundane and cheap wines. Wine just wasn't my thing. I drank mostly German beers. Next to the bottle were a nice wine glass and an opener. I opened the bottle, took a sip, and couldn't believe what I tasted; it was nectar of the gods.

The next day I went to every wine store I could find in San Francisco and bought every bottle of that 1968 vintage I could locate. When I asked for it in most wine stores, they just laughed at me and said it was sold out long ago. It was that good. I brought home thirteen full bottles and some half bottles. The full bottles cost $6.75 each and the half bottles cost $3.75 each, a lot of money for a bottle of wine in 1971. I later discovered that I was probably drinking the best domestic bottle of wine then available in America, and in the history of the Beaulieu Vineyards. It was their best year ever. That bottle sparked my lifelong interest in good wine and led me to eventually build a fine wine collection and cellar. Today, a newly-released bottle of BV private reserve costs well over $100, with great older bottles bringing hundreds of dollars at auction.

While on the west coast, I was also booked into P.J.'s club in Los Angeles, as the opening act for Martha Reeves and the Vandellas. Polydor was doing a good job of publicity for my album. They placed a large hand-painted copy of the album cover on a Sunset Boulevard billboard. The image was the same photo that is on the cover of this book, without the marijuana leaf of course. It was a real kick to see myself on the billboard as I drove past it. The photo was a Polaroid test shot taken by the well-known fashion photographer Joel Brodsky.

As part of the college tour, William Morris booked me into Brandeis University. My manager, Al, along with my bass player and drummer, drove with me to Brandeis for the date. It was pouring rain. The rain-soaked poster announced the late afternoon concert: Bobby Gosh and Carol Hall, $5.00 admission. My guys were setting up their equipment for the sound check. The opening singer, Carol Hall, whom I did not know, was running her sound check. Her songs were incredible and she had her own light man. That impressed the hell out of me.

On the increasingly-drenched poster, the $5.00 was now crossed out and replaced with $2.50. Shortly thereafter, I walked outside again to smoke a joint before the concert, and the $2.50 price was crossed out. The embarrassing word *Free* now inserted in its place.

Always in concerts, and most of the time in night clubs, I performed under the influence of marijuana. Marijuana allows me to dig emotionally deeper into the song that I am singing. I lose myself in the song. Nothing else matters. I am not conscious of the audience. I am transported totally into conveying the meaning of the song. To this day, I know I will give a greater performance under the influence of marijuana than without it.

Concert time! We had ten students in the audience, all of them seeming to be doing homework, etc. Carol came out and played her first beautiful song. Then a few people left. Carol played her next great song. A few more people left. Now there were about five people in the audience. I'm wondering if there was going to be anyone left in the audience for me, after Carol's next song. Carol played her third song, and a funny thing happened. More students started coming into the auditorium. People were leaving to find more students to bring to the concert. By the end of Carol's set, there was now a respectable size audience applauding excitedly. The lighting by Leonard Majzlin (an agent from our booking agency, William Morris) was excellent.

I was blown away by this young singer with her amazing songs. Carol's songs transport you into a beautiful nostalgic world, with lyrics like, "Nana loves irises, big, purple droop ones." I came on stage with a nicely controlled high, and my opening words were: "Wasn't she fucking incredible?" to which there was a loud roar of approval. I did my set, also beautifully lit by Leonard Majzlin, who remained in the lighting booth to help me out. When a singer/pianist performs on stage, the three most important things are a good piano, good sound, and good lighting. Together they give you the tools to command the audience's complete attention. You also must have good talent and good songs. Good talent and good songs with a bad piano and bad sound and lighting, however, is a recipe for disaster. Fortunately for this concert, I had everything covered. Thanks to Carol, I also had a respectably-sized audience.

Some months later, Carol and I appeared on the same bill at a concert in Central Park. Carol met Billi backstage and they hit it off right away. Years later Carol told me that she thought I was a mad, raving maniac at the Brandeis concert. After all, I was high and completely dressed in leather. But after meeting Billi and our three-year-old son Erik in Central Park, she thought maybe I was okay.

The Central Park concert was part of The Schaeffer Beer Music Festival. The master of ceremonies was well-known comedian Robert Klein. Besides Carol and me, the other performers on the bill were folksinger Tom Paxton, Bert Sommer, who was on Broadway in *Hair*, and Tony Joe White, who wrote, "A Rainy Night in Georgia" for Gladys Knight and the Pips.

Around this time, I was booked on the David Frost network television show to promote my album and had a ten-minute on-air conversation with David before playing and singing "If" on the show. A few months after the Central Park concert, Robert Klein was the guest host on the David Frost show. He asked me to come on the show as his guest. I told him I had appeared on the show a few months earlier. He said, "So what," and I did the show again.

Carol went on to have her songs recorded by Barbra Streisand, Tony Bennett, Big Bird on Sesame Street, Dolly Parton, and many others. She wrote the words and music for the hit Broadway show and movie, *The Best Little Whorehouse In Texas*. In fact, it was in our living room where she performed the songs before the musical debuted on Broadway. Carol's children and our children grew up together. And perhaps it was no surprise that Carol married her "light man," Leonard Majzlin, and they are living happily ever after. Carol and Leonard and Billi and I remain lifelong friends.

The touring, live concerts, and more national TV exposure gave me a taste of the big time rock and roll life, and best of all, introduced Billi and me to Carol and Leonard.

11

BIG BUCKS AND COMMERCIALS

After the touring, I came back to New York and resumed my gig at Jimmy Weston's. One of the frequent customers was an advertising executive, Angus McQueen, who worked for the D'Arcy Advertising Agency. One night he asked me if I did commercials. I mentioned some of the smaller commercials I had done while working at 12 East recording studios. Angus asked me to come to his office the next morning. I showed up promptly. He played me a General Tire commercial and said they weren't satisfied with the music. He asked me what I would do with it.

The thirty-second spot showed a tire rolling down a hill and all over the landscape. I thought for a few minutes and said I would create a lot of tension, motion, and excitement with a sixteen-piece string section and underline it with three electric rock and roll guitars and a rhythm section. Angus said time was of the essence and could I write the arrangement that day and record it the next? Yes, I said. I took a Moviola count to see what was happening at each frame and second of the commercial. The Moviola machine allowed you to start and stop the film at any individual frame. This allowed you to highlight the music to emphasize a particular part of the commercial.

At that time, before digital took over, to sync up music to film or video, you needed a book of charts to help you. I did not have the book, mainly because it was very expensive. I called my friend at 12 East Recording, where I was doing commercials, and he let me borrow his. I took the book home and wrote the music and arrangement. I called my copyist, Emile Charlap, whose office was on Times Square, and he stayed up all night copying the parts for the twenty-two-piece orchestra.

The next morning at 10:00 A.M., the arrangement parts were waiting for me on the conductor's stand at the recording studio. After one or two run-throughs the commercial was recorded and then mixed. New York studio musicians are so good that if there is a mistake, it's usually the fault of the arranger or copyist. There were no mistakes, so we were finished in less than an hour. Time in a top recording studio costs a lot of money. Musicians made over $100 an hour, the studio costs up to $300 an hour, and you had to pay for the copyist and recording tape. This session had cost approximately $3,500.

After the session, Angus invited me for lunch to discuss my payment. He said, "How about five for the creative fee?" This was the fee for writing the music and arrangement. I was quietly disappointed, thinking he meant $500, when I always had made at least $750 on smaller commercials. I said OK, thinking that I would get more work from him. Angus then said, "Great, $5,000 for the creative fee." I almost fell off my chair. My pay as musician, conductor, and contractor was about $500, so all in all I made about $5,500 in the last twenty-four hours for about ten hours of work.

I went home and told Billi, "I'll never play in a night club again. From here on, I'm going to write and sing commercials." Having just successfully tasted a big league national TV commercial, I now knew where the real money was.

I gave Jimmy Weston a three-month notice and thanked him for the wonderful two years I spent playing in his night club. Jimmy understood, and we remained good friends until his death years later.

Shortly after I gave my notice, Angus was sitting in Weston's with a beautiful woman and I stopped by his table. The woman was Ford model Jodi Wexler, and they had just returned from a commercial shoot in Germany for Lufthansa Airlines. Angus said Jodi was a singer, so I invited her to come up on the stage and sing during my next show. The room got totally quiet when she sang her first song, and the crowd loved her. Whenever Angus and Jodi came into Weston's I would invite her to sing. She also sang background vocals on my first Polydor album, which was in production at the time.

I did more commercials for Angus and he eventually married Jodi. We all became good friends. Jodi went on to play a major part in the movie *The Love Machine*. She also wrote songs. My second Polydor album was due in 1972 and I had no new songs, so I collaborated with Jodi to write all the songs for the album, titled *Mother Motor*. Jodi was a prolific lyricist, and came up with the concept for the album, which was country rock.

Polydor and Jon Sagen, my A&R man, were going through some difficult times, so my album got lost in the shuffle. Angus and Jodi moved to Oklahoma City where Angus built an advertising agency which now has five offices in major cities, employing 250 people. Jodi continued to write songs, play guitar, and make beautiful paintings. They had three children. Sadly, Jodi died in 2013. I will always remember the great times we all had together. Angus and Jodi's love affair was so deep that immediately after her death, Angus acted on his promise to her that he would keep her memory alive. In September 2015, Angus released an incredibly beautiful two-volume boxed set of books and videos. It is a complete record of Jodi's wonderful and creative life, as a model, movie star, songwriter, musician, painter, loving wife, and mother. Believe it or not, the packaged set weighs in at sixty-three pounds. As a collector of fine books, I am astounded at this amazing feat Angus accomplished. He will release a professionally produced documentary of Jodi's life in 2017. Angus and I still keep in touch with each other.

I began doing a lot of commercials. I made a demo reel of the commercials I had done and dropped it off at various big advertising agencies in Manhattan. Roy Eaton, the music producer at Benton & Bowles, hired me to work on Post cereals' Saturday morning children's commercials. I had joined the Screen Actors Guild, or SAG, which is the union that represents singers on television commercials, and AFTRA, which is the union that represented singers on radio commercials at that time. They have recently merged. I wrote the songs, arranged and produced the recording sessions, and sang on all the Post cereal commercials for about six years. I became the signature voice for Post Honeycomb cereal.

Singing the commercial was where the money was. I was the first guy in New York to sing in a rough Joe Cocker type of voice in commercials, instead of the pretty, standard commercial male voice. I was one of the writers on the Honeycomb Hideout commercials and sang on all the spots. After a few years, they used that title line only—"Come to the Honey Comb Hideout,"with me singing it—to open every Honeycomb cereal commercial they made for another five years. I collected a total of around $100,000 in residuals for the six-year run of the Honeycomb Hideout series of commercials alone. What a great way to make a living.

Television commercials ran in thirteen-week cycles. The lead singer would get about $350 each time a thirty-second spot was shown for the first thirteen times. After that, it would go down to around $250 for the next thirteen times and so on. After the first cycle, the residual would start at the top rate again. The money could add up quickly. Billi and I would lie in bed Saturday mornings and flip the channels to watch my commercials running. I remember getting out of bed on some Saturday mornings in our apartment in Manhattan and realizing I had just made $3,500 lying in bed. My decision to pursue commercial work was definitely paying off.

The payment for writing a song for a commercial was earned differently. When an advertising agency needed a new song for a client, they usually went to five jingle writers and gave them each $5,000 to write a song and make a demo. They would play the demos for the client and the client would choose the winner. I received $5,000 to write a song for Newport filter cigarettes, along with four other writers. Newport picked my song and I was chosen to sing it. The money would be phenomenal: $25,000 for writing the song (creative fee) and singing residuals for years! I could easily make six figures for any cigarette commercial. On January 2, 1971, three weeks after my commercial was chosen, however, the government banned all television cigarette advertising. Another near miss. Today, my principles and disdain for smoking would not allow me to do a smoking commercial.

I did commercials for Pepsi Cola, Burger King, Arby's, and many others. I sang the Burger King "Have It Your Way" commercial in my rough voice and arranged a large orchestra version with strings. In the late 1970s, the advertising legend George Lois wrote and produced an Arby's commercial. A friend of mine was working for him and suggested that I sing it. I was living in Vermont and flew to New York for the recording session. I arrived at the recording studio for the night time session and four backup singers were there. Throughout the whole session, the backup singers were trying to get George Lois to pick one of them to sing the solo, which is where the most money is earned. New York commercial singers were a cut throat group because the financial stakes were so high. I found out, through my friend, that they had recorded one of the backup singers the next day, singing the solo I had sung. A few days later, they chose my version. I earned about $17,000 for my night's work, including all residuals. That was the last national television commercial I ever did.

Because I was living fulltime in Vermont and no longer had a manager in New York (Al and I had amicably split up since it was no longer economically feasible for me to employ him), I disappeared from the New York commercial scene. I had no regrets and was thankful for the experience and the money.

An advertising agency in Randolph, Vermont, hired me when they needed music for their commercials in the late 1970s. I found a good recording studio named Philo, near Burlington, and used it to record the music. The agency asked me to write a commercial for the Vermont Yankee nuclear power plant in Vernon, Vermont. I had mixed feelings about doing it until I discovered that 80 percent of the power used in Vermont at that time came from Vermont Yankee. As a heavy user of electricity, I figured that I would be a hypocrite if I didn't accept the job. The campaign, "We Light Up Your Life," (don't laugh) was meant to give nuclear power a better image in Vermont.

I wrote and recorded the song and it was a success. A few months later, I got a call from a writer at *Rolling Stone*. He asked me if I was aware that Bonnie Raitt played a concert the night before at the Sugarbush ski area. He said that she mentioned my name as the writer of the pronuclear power commercial that was being widely played on radio and television in Vermont. Raitt was a staunch antinuclear advocate and went on about how bad a guy I was for writing the commercial.

The writer asked if I had any comment. I told him I certainly did and he should turn on his tape recorder. If he was going to quote me, he should make sure the quote was accurate, or I would sue him and *Rolling Stone*. I said, "Tell Bonnie Raitt that she is a fucking hypocrite because her microphone, guitar, amplifiers, and spot lights were sucking the electricity from the Vermont Yankee nuclear power plant. Without it, none of the thousands of her fans sitting on the side of the mountain would have heard her chastising me, or heard her music, or a single word she was singing." The writer thanked me, hung up, and *Rolling Stone* never printed a word about it.

Residuals for long past commercials can have long legs, and can pop up at any time. A few years ago, I got a call from the producers of the animated TV show "Family Guy." They said they used four seconds of a thirty-five-year old Post Cereal commercial song, "Honeycomb's Big, Yeh, Yeh, Yeh," which I co-wrote. They asked where to send the residual check. The two co-writers and I split $12,000.

12

VERMONT

In the fall of 1971, Billi was pregnant with our daughter Kristina. We wanted to buy a vacation house. We had skied in Vermont since we were married and decided to look there. I had been booked for a concert date at Goddard College a few months before and really liked the area between White River Junction and Montpelier, which I drove through on my way from Manhattan to Goddard. We took a fall foliage trip to Vermont in October. We looked at about thirty houses all over the state and found a three-year-old small ranch house on six acres. It didn't seem like much, but the windows looked out on uninterrupted fields and mountains in nearly every direction—with a seventy-mile view to the south, all the way to the Killington ski area. We figured we could make the house into anything we wanted, but could never find a more spectacular view. After we bought it, we went to Vermont whenever we could, but lived in our Manhattan apartment until 1975.

We bought the house from Dan and Viola Chase. Dan was a retired farmer and former state legislator. Viola was a housewife. They were already spending winters in Tampa, Florida. They decided to sell the Vermont retirement house they had just built a few years earlier and live fulltime in Florida. Of the hundreds of acres Dan farmed, he picked the highest spot with the most spectacular view to build their 24 X 40 foot ranch house.

I began to attend country auctions and decided to write a song about them. I realized that Billi and I moved to Vermont to live the good life; and Dan and Viola sold their house and country lifestyle and moved to Tampa to live the good life. Different strokes for different folks, but definitely the seed of a song.

I combined this thought with the auction idea and wrote the song "Two for a Dollar." It has always been one of my favorite songs, and I recorded it for my third album, *Sitting In The Quiet*. The good life idea became the punch line for the end of the song. The country singer Bobby Bare also recorded a great version on his *Hard Times Hungrys* album. My friend Leonard Majzlin shot some footage at a Vermont country auction. He edited it to the song, making a charming film that he gave me as a gift.

Two for a Dollar

Last Saturday morning I shut off the alarm
Drove out in the valley to old Dan Cook's farm
A sign on the fencepost put up with one nail
Read 10:00 A.M. sharp—big public sale.

At least forty people were out in the yard
Lookin' for bargains, they were dealin' real hard
To buy up the pieces and find out the worth
Of fifty-years livin' so close to the earth.

Chorus:
Who'll give me five, I got five now who'll give me ten?
I'll call out the numbers and you just say when
For a lifetime of mem'ries, some happy some sad
Two for a dollar, the price sure ain't bad.

No bids for the carriage rotting out by the shed
The one that they drove on the night they were wed
Five bucks for the brass bed, a little bit worn
Not much for the place where the five kids were born.

And the old parlor piano still sounded alright
Just as good as it did many a Saturday night
And the big round oak table where dinner was laid
Brought almost as much as the tiffany shade.

Chorus:
Who'll give me five, I got five now who'll give me ten?
I'll call out the numbers and you just say when
For a lifetime of mem'ries, some happy some sad
Two for a dollar, the price sure ain't bad
But old Dan needs the money, so he and his wife
Can move down to Tampa, and live the good life.

In 1973 Al got me a $50,000 record deal with ABC Paramount Records for one album. Chuck Gregory, the A&R man at Paramount, suggested Lynn Barkley to produce the album, so I hired him. I had produced my first two Polydor albums myself. I wrote all the songs for the Paramount album. The album was titled *Sitting In The Quiet*. The William Morris Agency booked me into the Troubadour nightclub in Hollywood to promote the album in 1973, when it was released. I was the opening act for Billy Joel, who already had his first big hit with "Piano Man." For new and upcoming musicians, the Troubadour was the most important club you could perform in on the west coast. Elton John, James Taylor, Carole King, and just about all the great singer/songwriters of the seventies started there.

At the same time I was producing *Sitting In The Quiet*, Paramount Pictures, the parent company of Paramount Records, had a new movie coming out called *Bang The Drum Slowly*, starring newcomer, Robert De Niro. I had $5,000 left in my recording budget. Paramount Pictures asked me to sing and record the title song of the movie, which would be inserted into the film and also be on my album. The song was based on an old folk song, with additions by two other writers. It was a good song and I liked it.

After I recorded the song, the movie company argued with the record company for three weeks as to who would pay the $10,000 cost to insert and lay the song over the closing credits of the completed film. Finally, the record company said it would pay the cost and notified the movie company. The movie company responded, "You are too late. We printed the copies of the film yesterday without the song." The sheet music was already printed with a picture from the film on the cover, stating that I sang the song in the movie. It was the only song on my album that I didn't write. If my version of the song had been in the movie, it might have become a hit due to the exposure: The film was successful and launched De Niro's career. Another near miss, but the album did eventually give me the biggest hit song of my career. One of my songs on the album, "A Little Bit More," became a worldwide hit three years later in 1976, when Dr. Hook recorded it.

In March of 1972 our daughter Kristina was born. Billi and I were spending more and more time at our house in Vermont. In 1973, we put the first addition on the Vermont house: a small office for me, a mud room entrance, and a two-car garage. Al would use our Manhattan apartment for an office while we were in Vermont. If a commercial job came in, Al would call me and I'd hop on a plane immediately and could be in New York in a few hours if necessary. I was within an hour's drive to three airports, so commuting to New York by plane was convenient. This routine continued for the next few years.

When our building was turned into condominiums, we could have bought our apartment for $175,000, which was the insider's price. We could have flipped it for double that price, which was the going retail rate for an apartment of that size, or rented it for additional income. We decided to not buy it and eventually moved out, which in hindsight was a stupid move. Today, I would value that apartment at $2.5 million. Another near miss.

In 1975, Billi, Erik, Kristina and I moved from our Manhattan apartment to live full time in Vermont. The day we moved, the weather was nice in Manhattan, but as soon as we reached the Vermont border, we were in the middle of a snow and ice storm. I was driving the twenty-four-foot rental truck with a friend, Greg Sharrow. Billi followed with Erik and a huge ficus tree in our 1974 Volkswagen. Krissy and our 1968 Cadillac Eldorado were already in Vermont. When we came to a slight hill about two miles from our house, the truck started sliding backwards. Luckily, I was able to back it into a farmer's driveway. The farmer gave me permission to leave the truck there until the next morning. Greg and I squeezed into the trusty VW, which slowly got us all home.

As we could afford it, Billi and I planned and added on to the house to reflect the lifestyle we wanted to live. We are our own decorators, and could not live in a home decorated with someone else's taste. We had an architect draw up the elevations of what we planned to build. This way, the house would look designed instead of cobbled together. Over the years, we bought more land, and built additions, as we could afford them. We ended up with a nearly 9,000-square-foot house on twenty acres with three ponds. For the additions, we repurposed many architectural antiques that we picked up at auctions and antique stores: stained glass windows; lighting fixtures; rare woods that were milled, dried, and stored for about 100 years; a 1909 tin ceiling, 1929 art deco lights; 1879 oak pocket doors; 1875 oak shelves from a pharmacy that we used for a library, and antique bannisters and railings. Walk into the bathroom off our bedroom and it's as if you're in a barbershop circa 1919, with all the sinks, cabinets, and mirrors just as they appeared in an old newspaper clipping about the shop. The clipping hangs framed on the bathroom wall. Billi and I love the Victorian era. We couldn't find a Victorian house with a view, so we bought the view and built the house.

That same year, Al got me a record deal for four singles with RCA Records. The A&R man who signed me was Neil Portnow, who later became the director and president of the Grammy Awards. I recorded four of my songs in Hollywood with Steve Dorff, as arranger and producer of the sessions. His son is Stephen Dorff, the well-known movie actor. RCA released a single, nothing much happened with it, and that was the end of that. Neil then suggested that I write a song for a CBS movie of the week starring Suzanne Somers. I was told that Peter Matz, a well-known arranger and composer, was scoring the movie. The story evolved around a songwriter and they needed a strong song—it was critical to the storyline of the entire movie. Peter had taken a few shots at the song, but the producers were not satisfied with the results.

They sent the script to me overnight. I spent the next three days at the grand piano, which was squeezed into my small office in Vermont. In one scene of the movie, the songwriter appears in a suit of armor on a beautiful white horse, as he attempts to woo his girlfriend, played by Suzanne Somers. I wrote the song with lyrics fashioned after a fairy tale and titled it "You Made A Believer Out Of Me," which was a line in the script.

Al and I flew to Hollywood to present the song to the movie producer. A small upright piano and a floor lamp with a single bare light bulb were the only items on the sound stage of the movie lot. Once again, the scene made me feel like I was in an old Woody Allen movie. The producer arrived and introduced himself. I sat down at the piano and played and sang the song. As the song progressed, the smile on the producer's face grew wider. When I finished the song, he said, "We'll be in touch shortly."

When Al and I returned to our room at the Beverly Hills Hotel, there was a note under the door to call the producer. They bought the song for $10,000. One of my lines in the song became the title of the movie, *Happily Ever After*. I stayed in Hollywood for a few more days to coach Suzanne, a lovely, down-to-earth person, how to sing the song. Peter Matz did the arrangement for the orchestra and I played the piano at the recording session.

Even though I was living fulltime in rural Vermont, I was participating in the national music scene. This was possible because, at that time, Al was still representing me from New York. This allowed me to straddle two very different worlds.

13

BECOMING A STUDENT OF THE UNIVERSE

I was now living full-time in Vermont, far from the city lights. I became closer to nature and the marvels and wonders of the star-filled, nighttime sky, which became my gateway to the universe. Having more free time to think, I began to pay attention to the hypocrisy of religions. The way the Catholic church treated Galileo was one of the major reasons I came to realize that I had absolutely no tolerance for religion. How could anyone respect a religion that almost burned a genius at the stake, just because he looked through his telescope and figured out that the Earth revolved around the Sun (heliocentric system) and not vice versa (geocentric system) as Catholics were taught to believe? And then took another 359 years until the pope admitted the church was wrong? Here was a religion of hundreds of millions of people almost condemning to death one of the greatest astronomers of all time because of its belief in a fairy tale.

According to Wikipedia, in 1633 the Roman Inquisition tried Galileo and found him "vehemently suspect of heresy," and sentenced him to indefinite imprisonment for his heliocentric belief. Some philosophers of the day who opposed his discoveries had refused even to look through a telescope. He was ordered to abandon completely his opinion that the Sun stands still at the center of our Solar System and the Earth moves around it. He was forced to recant his scientific findings to avoid being burned at the stake. He was kept under house arrest until his death in 1642.

On October 31, 1992, Pope John Paul II acknowledged that the Roman Catholic church had erred in condemning Galileo for his discovery. Stephen Hawking declared Galileo to be the person most responsible for the birth of modern science. Einstein called him the father of modern science.

Learning about the Galileo affair was the final straw in my questioning of religion and was responsible for the birth of my atheism. The treatment of Galileo demonstrated for me the hypocrisy of religion far more seriously than my experience with the "parking lot hypocrites" of my youth, when I attended church with my grandmother.

I became a student of the universe.

Clockwise from left:
Johannes Gosch (Bobby's grandfather),
Dorothea Vogt Gosch (Bobby's grandmother),
Ursula Gosch (Bobby's paternal aunt),
and Hans Gosch (Bobby's father), 1914

Bobby, *bottom left*, with his parents, Hans
and Margaret, and brother, Fred, 1945

Left to right: Kristina, Billi, Erik, and Bobby, Vermont, 1974

Left to right: Erik, Bobby, Kristina, and Billi, Vermont, 1975

Bottom to top: Erik, Kristina, Billi, and Bobby, 2003

Sammy Cahn with Bobby at the piano, 1965

Left to right: Bobby, Sheila MacRae, Gordon MacRae, and Joan Crawford
at Billy Reed's Little Club, 1966

Left to right: Steve Lawrence, Paul Anka (hidden), Bobby, Jack Jones, and Jayne Morgan on the "Tonight Show," Christmas Eve 1969. (Photo taken from TV screen).

Bobby receiving a gold record for "A Little Bit More," 1977

Paul Anka and Bobby by the pool of the El San Juan Hotel in Puerto Rico, 1968

Suzanne Somers and Bobby in Hollywood for the CBS TV movie of the week, 1975

Left to right: Milt Hinton, Paul Anka (dancing on the piano), and Bobby, 1968

Left to right: Bob Mann, Bobby, Denny Seiwell, and Don Payne,
recording first Polydor album, 1971

Bobby recording first Polydor album, 1971

Bobby conducting the string section for first Polydor album, 1971

Carol Hall and Bobby in concert at Chandler Center for the Arts, 2003
Credit: Jeb Wallace-Brodeur

Bobby in concert at Chandler Center for the Arts, 2007
Credit: Bob Eddy

Bobby in the control room of his home recording studio
Credit: Tim Calabro

Bobby composing at his piano
Credit: Toby Talbot

14

A LITTLE BIT MORE

In 1973, I wrote my worldwide hit "A Little Bit More" (for my ABC Paramount album, *Sitting in the Quiet*) at the grand piano in our Manhattan apartment in less than an hour. As I was writing it, the song seemed to be dictated to me from elsewhere. Many songwriters of successful songs have expressed a similar experience. I believe that the quicker the song comes to you, the better the song is. The longer I labor on a song, the more difficult it is to write. My song, "Killed by *The Wall Street Journal*," which I wrote for my deceased stockbroker friend Eddy Stern, took over forty years to write. I had the title for forty years and had many false starts. Once I decided to really write it a few years ago, I finished it in a few days and consider it a good song.

My process for writing a song usually begins with a title, which can be the song's subject. It will be the hook of the song also. A *hook* is a repeated musical and lyrical phrase that worms its way into the listener's mind. The more the listener hears the hook, the more it stays stuck. A good hook, or earworm, is the basis of a hit song.

A song is composed of a verse or verses leading to the chorus, which usually contains the hook. The chorus is repeated after each verse and usually repeated at least once at the end of the song. If I read or hear something in the media which sounds like a hook, I will write it down on a scrap of paper. I have hundreds of titles that I never developed into a song. Sometimes a hook or a title will just pop into my mind for reasons I do not know. I get many great hook ideas, however, under the influence of marijuana. It may sound far-fetched, but maybe I'm communing in some way with the frequency waves of the universe.

I most often write the lyric first. When I get a good idea for a lyric, I think about it for a few days and formulate it in my mind. When I have a pretty good first draft, I will sit at the piano and compose a melody that fits the lyric and emphasizes the hook. As Sammy Cahn once told me, the lyric must "sing well," meaning the words can't sound awkward and must flow comfortably off the tongue when they are sung to a melody.

If I am commissioned to write a song, the lyric must reflect what the client wants me to convey. A good example of this is the clock song "Welcome to Our World of Toys," which I wrote for the FAO Schwarz toy store to bring the clocktower to life. The key words I used included clock, tick-tock, toys, and girls and boys. Commercial clients sometimes supply the lyric and hire me to write the music.

People would ask Sammy Cahn, "What comes first, the music or the lyrics?" Sammy would answer, "The phone call." The phone call would either be from Frank Sinatra, requesting Sammy to write a song for Frank's newest album, or a movie producer, requesting a song for a new movie.

People would ask Sammy, "What's most important, the music or the lyrics?" Sammy, a lyricist, would respond, "Did you ever hear anyone walking down the street humming the lyric?"

Then one day in May of 1976, the *real* Hook appeared in my life. The phone rang in Vermont. The caller was the producer of the popular recording group Dr. Hook— appropriately named, as they were masters of singing hit songs with great hooks. He asked me to listen to my song "A Little Bit More," which Dr. Hook had just recorded. I was very impressed. Many times when I heard one of my songs recorded, I wasn't too impressed with the results. He told me that his friend Shel Silverstein found my 1973 album, *Sitting in the Quiet*, in a thirty-nine-cent remainder bin and suggested that Dr. Hook record my song. Shel had written many of the group's hits including "On the Cover of *Rolling Stone*," and "Sylvia's Mother." While he is best remembered today as a poet and writer of children's books, Shel was also a well-known cartoonist in *Playboy*. Because of Shel's generous suggestion, I had the biggest hit song of my career. I wrote him a thank-you letter, but never received a reply. One thing I learned is that once a good song is floating around out there, you never know where it may end up. Sammy Cahn once told me, "A good song is always a good song, whether it becomes a hit or not."

Once a song is recorded, anyone else has the right to record it too, as long as they request a license from the publisher. I was the writer and publisher for "A Little Bit More." The producer said my song was going to be Dr. Hook's new single and he was requesting a percentage of the publishing rights in return for recording and releasing it. This was a common practice in the music business. A song's income is shared as follows: 50 percent to the writer or writers, and 50 percent to the publisher or publishers. The producer was requesting half of the publishing income. I agreed. In exchange, the producer got me a $50,000 contract for him to produce an album of my songs for Capitol Records, which was also Dr. Hook's record label. It seemed like a no-brainer to me.

In June of 1976 "A Little Bit More" began to climb the charts. It became number eleven in America and hit number two in England, just below the number-one hit "Don't Go Breaking My Heart" by Elton John and Kiki Dee. It was on the British charts for twenty-six weeks. It was also a hit in Sweden, Denmark, Australia, and many other countries, thus becoming a worldwide hit.

The producer took me to the Nashville studio where Dr. Hook recorded, and where we recorded the first four songs for my Capitol Records album. I had to fly to Nashville again to re-record just one line in one of the songs. He was a good producer and a perfectionist. Capitol released one single of mine. The producer never finished my album, for reasons unknown, and pocketed my remaining production money. Capitol suspended me for not delivering the album and that was the end of that. I stopped paying the producer's company his share of the royalties for "A Little Bit More" and they sued me. After a few years, we settled out of court. The Capitol Records deal could have been a huge boost to my career but it turned out to be just another near miss.

When *Sitting In The Quiet* was first released in 1973, "A Little Bit More" could not be played on the radio because of the sexual connotations of the lyrics, even though it was the best song on the album. Just three years later, however, the 1970s was in full swing (and full of swingers). To borrow a cliché, the 1970s was all about sex, drugs, and rock and roll. As a result, radio censors were more lax, so more suggestive lyrics could be heard on the radio. And Dr. Hook was able to make it a hit, thanks in part to the suggestive images of the song's hook.

At the peak of the hit in America, I got a call from the popular TV show "Tony Orlando and Dawn." They requested a license to sing the song on their show. But they needed to change the first line of the chorus from "When your body's had enough of me" to "When you've had enough of me." I said they could not change the lyric and must sing it as I wrote it. That was a problem, they said. They already taped the show for broadcast on the following Saturday night. I could have stopped them from using the song, but my manager and I decided to take the $3,000-TV-performance money and run. I guess I sold out, but it was national TV exposure for the song. Radio could play the song, but the TV censors still said no to the suggestive lyric.

Today my lyric is mild compared to the current hits of the pop music world. Take, for example, CeeLo Green, who had an uncensored YouTube internet hit a few years ago that helped launch his career. The title of the song was "Fuck You." They did change the title to "Forget You" for radio and TV play.

A Little Bit More

Come on over here and lay by my side
I've got to be touchin' you
Let me rub your tired shoulders
The way I used to do

Look into my eyes and give me that smile
The one that always turns me on
And let me take your hair down
'Cause we're stayin' up to greet the sun

Chorus:
And when your body's had enough of me
And I'm layin' flat out on the floor
When you think I've loved you all I can
I'm gonna love you a little bit more

Got to say a few things that have been on my mind
And you know where my mind has been
I guess I learned my lesson
And now's the time to begin

So if you're feelin' alright and you're ready for me
I know that I'm ready for you
We better get it on now
'Cause we got a whole life to live through
(*Repeat chorus*)

15

A GROWING PROBLEM

Throughout my over sixty years of consuming marijuana, I almost always bought it illegally off the street. Occasionally I got a gift from a friend. In New York in the 1960s and 1970s, it was very easy to find; it usually came from Mexico (Acapulco Gold). After moving to Vermont, my source was either Mexican or Vermont grown. Vermont pot was inconsistent with varying degrees of potency, and sometimes hard to find.

There was a lot of land around our house in Vermont. In the spring of 1973 I decided to cultivate a few marijuana plants for my own use. One day my neighbor knocked on the door and said his three sons found my plants. I told him that I would make the plants disappear immediately. I moved the plants and never heard another complaint from him. Realizing I needed a new and more-secure place for my experiment in growing grass, I contacted a friend of mine who had a house off the grid, high on top of a mountain, about twenty miles from my house. He told me I could grow some pot on his property. Another friend of mine and I planted a bunch of seeds in an opening on his land, which was quite remote. We fertilized and watered the plants regularly. Around September, I noticed helicopters flying low and found out that they were police looking for marijuana plants.

Concerned, my friend and I decided to harvest our crop. Early one evening we went to our marijuana garden in his pickup truck and cut all the plants. His truck had a cab cover on it, so the crop could not be seen. We drove cautiously through the town of Randolph after dark, driving just two blocks from the police station. When we got to my house, we hung the plants upside-down to dry on the second floor of the garage. We grew the plants for our own use only. The potency was pretty mild because the plants had almost no buds on them due to our early harvest. Basically, we didn't know what we were doing. We didn't know about male and female plants and buds, among other things. When I think back on this whole escapade, I realize that my friend and I could still be in jail if we had been caught while driving our load through town.

A year or two later I met another friend, who also lived off the grid, way out in the woods with no electricity or running water. He was very knowledgeable about growing marijuana and ginseng and made a proposition: If I fronted him the money for fertilizer each spring, he would give me a nice amount of pot each fall when he harvested his crop. I took him up on the deal, which went on for a few years. The marijuana he grew was excellent (giving a nice high) and he would also throw in some ginseng and some home-brewed mead that he made with marijuana.

A few years later this friend and another friend of his were stopped by the police for driving too slowly on their return trip from Ohio, where they were apparently selling marijuana. My friend looked like a mountain man with his extreme beard, and the police searched the car for over two hours. They found a small amount of marijuana and $85,000 in cash hidden in the car. My friend somehow got off with no jail time, but his friend got about four years in prison for having a previous marijuana arrest. Needless to say, the police confiscated the cash. I sent a character reference letter to the judge for my friend and I like to think that it helped him.

In the last few years, all the pot I buy is medical marijuana sold on the black market. I can get all the 20 percent THC medical marijuana I want. Some licensed medical growers in some states grow more than they need and sell it to dealers who sell it on the street to customers like me. Also, some medical marijuana patients resell some of their pot that they buy legally. The good news is that the marijuana is consistent and potent, with the THC content printed on the package. The bad news: It is expensive.

Vermont legislators approved medical marijuana in 2004, but only for cancer, HIV, multiple sclerosis, severe pain, and a few other things. I don't qualify, so I must continue to buy illegally. The present political climate in Vermont, however, portends toward some form of legalizing recreational marijuana by 2018 or shortly thereafter. I am patiently awaiting that day.

16

A MANHATTAN DISCO IN VERMONT

One day in late 1975, I was driving through Randolph and noticed a "For Sale" sign on an old gas station. I called the owner, Cities Service, in Oklahoma, and was told that the price was $11,000. I asked how I could see the inside of the building and the owner told me to break the padlock and go in. My carpenter and I broke the lock and entered the building, only to be confronted by a leaking roof, buckled floors, and piles of wet and moldy clothing from the last tenant who ran a thrift shop. But the foundation was solid and it had 3,000 square feet of space. I told Cities Service, if they cut down a tree that was about to fall on the building and filled the empty 8,000-gallon gas tanks with sand, as required by state law, I would buy the property. They agreed, and we closed on the deal.

Since moving to Vermont, Billi and I had begun to collect antiques. We stored them on the second floor of the garage we built in 1973. One night after a dinner party at our house, we went upstairs in the garage to show our guests some new antique acquisitions. As we all walked to the center of the floor, it caved in and all the antiques slid toward the center of the floor. The floor sank just shy of the cars below. I called the carpenter at midnight to come over and shore up the floor, which he did with a house jack. It was clear we needed a new home for our growing collection.

Billi and I decided to open an antique store in our new building and empty out the inventory in the garage. Antiques were plentiful in Vermont at that time and I enjoyed going to auctions and hunting them down. I began to restore the building and we opened six months later. Our antique shop, called Antiques Unlimited, specialized in antique wood stoves—it was during the energy crisis. We sold more than thirty stoves in just a few months. We heated the building with wood stoves. When an antique dealer came into the store, I would tell him, "The more you buy, the bigger the discount." I had return customers who would buy enough to fill a sixteen-foot truck.

My pot growing friend and I were sitting in the antique store one afternoon. I told him I always wanted to open a restaurant, as I had spent many years early in my career performing in them. He said, "You're sitting in it." I said, "What do you mean?" He said, "This is the perfect place for a restaurant." The building was the best location in town.

So Billi and I built a kitchen addition. The restaurant opened on July 4, 1976. We called the place Victoria's, after Queen Victoria, because the 100-seat restaurant was completely furnished in Victorian antiques. For the first few months customers could buy the tables and chairs they sat on, the dishes they ate off of, and other antiques in the restaurant. This became impractical because as time went on it was more difficult to replace the items, so we abandoned that idea.

That summer "A Little Bit More" was climbing the charts around the world. Capitol Records released my first single record, "Fifteen Shades of The Rainbow." Billi and I decided to have a party at Victoria's to celebrate our good fortune. A friend of mine,

Seymour Holtzman, flew himself and ten Capitol Records executives to the party in his private plane. I made a tape loop of "A Little Bit More" being sung in over a dozen languages from the various countries in which it was a hit.

Victoria's stayed open for eleven years. We had as many as twenty employees at one time. The chef managed the kitchen and we had another manager for the front of the house. Billi and I never worked there, but she did the payroll and I paid the bills once a week. It never showed a profit, but was a lot of fun and very convenient for entertaining guests. You entered the restaurant through a glass-walled vestibule lined with plants. There were three dining rooms and a bar room with a stained glass ceiling circa 1849. The walls were decorated with over 100 antique Victorian prints, and all the lighting fixtures were authentic Victorian. You never knew who would pop into the place. One day two limos pulled up and newscaster David Brinkley and his entire family came into the restaurant after a day of skiing. David said they loved the food and the atmosphere.

With help from a New York City disco designer, I built a state-of-the-art discotheque in the center room with lights hidden in the wall openings. The dance floor could be viewed from the whole restaurant. The ceiling in the center dancing room was seventeen feet high with a DJ booth on a balcony. The room was used for dining until 10:00 on Friday and Saturday nights. Then the tables would be cleared from the room, the colored disco ceiling lights would dance on the floor, the lights in the wall openings would turn on and go through their cycles, and a song like "Sara" by Fleetwood Mac would flow through the super sound system. Our friends Harry and Katharine Diamant, who were excellent disco dancers, would take to the floor. Harry would twirl Katharine above his head, John Travolta style, and by the second song, the dance floor would be packed with happy dancers. It was a small Manhattan-type disco in Randolph, Vermont—a unique and magical experience. Everybody loved it.

Our son Erik, who was about twelve at the time, observed the DJs we hired. One day he said he could do the job and proved it to me. Shortly after that, he became the DJ. One Saturday night when the dance floor was packed, the music suddenly stopped. I climbed the ladder to the balcony to see what was going on. Erik was curled up on the floor sound asleep. Luckily, we were never arrested for abusing child labor laws.

In 1986 a recession was looming and Victoria's was hemorrhaging money. We went in debt over $65,000 in the last year to keep it open. On January 1, 1987, we closed the restaurant and put it up for sale. We had a buyer for the building within two weeks, but it took over a year and a half before we could close on the sale due to a cloud on the title. After all the debts were paid, we cleared a tidy profit on the building's sale and the sale of the restaurant equipment at auction. We kept the stained glass ceiling, which was over the bar, and some important art works and antiques. We incorporated them into our home, where they remain today.

I made the disco lights and equipment portable so Erik could expand the DJ business he had started. While we paid Erik's college tuition at Champlain College in Burlington, Vermont, he paid for all his other college expenses, his apartment, and car with the money he made on weekends with the portable disco. Erik was born to be an entrepreneur. In 1986, at eighteen, he held down three jobs. He worked in a video store, was a DJ at Victoria's and other restaurants, and wholesaled sneakers out of a tent with his friend Pember Dupras. He made $23,000 that year and bought a new 1986 Cadillac Cimarron with his own money.

While at college, he and his friend Pember published *The Vermont Wedding Guide*, which complimented his DJ business. Upon completing college, he started a business selling his own brand of mattresses through classified ads in three New England states. In 2003 he began working for Cott Beverages. Today he is vice president of sales for the United States. He and his wife, Martha, have three children, Max, Simon, and Maeve.

Our daughter Kristina's first job was as a bus girl at Victoria's. She studied French in high school. After high school, she spent a year as an exchange student in Belgium, where she became fluent in Dutch. From the age of sixteen, she spent the next six summers in St. Tropez as an au pair for a Manhattan couple's two children. Kris went on to major in French and art at the University of Vermont (UVM) in Burlington. She spent one semester in Florence, Italy, studying at the SACI art school, where she became fluent in Italian. Learning languages is a piece of cake for Kris.

While Kristina was studying at SACI, Billi and I visited the Vatican and the homes of cardinals. I was shocked that the popes and cardinals built these monuments to themselves and accumulated vast troves of art and illustrated manuscripts, instead of spending the wealth on the poor. Their hypocritical history of mistresses, sex, and the later cover-ups of pedophilia reinforced my atheism.

After graduation from UVM in 1996, Kris was the au pair for a French couple in Paris for a year. She was often told she spoke French without an American accent. She moved to Chicago in 1997, where she made art while working at various jobs. She received her MFA from Columbia College in Chicago in 2010. She was an adjunct professor at Columbia and a teaching artist in the Chicago public school system until she moved back to Vermont in November 2015 with her fiancé Matt Thomas.

Of course, Billi and I are extremely proud of Kristina and Erik. And we'd like to think that, just maybe, Victoria's had a tiny part in instilling them with their great work ethic.

17

BEYOND WORDS

In the 1970s, I started reading some of the books by Carlos Castaneda, an anthropologist and writer who wrote about his experiences during a five-year apprenticeship with Don Juan Matus, a seventy-year-old Mexican-Yaqui Indian sorcerer. Don Juan used peyote, among other hallucinogens, to open the doors of perception to a world of "non-ordinary reality." I became interested in the power of peyote.

One day in the early 1980s, an acquaintance asked me if I wanted to purchase some fresh peyote. I jumped at the chance and came home with three or four green tomato look-alikes. There were white hairs growing out of the top, which I was told contained strychnine. I was instructed to remove the white hairs and eat the peyote like you would eat a tomato.

A few nights later, Billi and I had some friends over to our house for drinks. We were going to Victoria's for dinner later. I decided to eat some peyote. It was a beautiful evening and we watched the sun go down from the patio. After about an hour, the peyote kicked in and I began hallucinating. I realized that I had completely lost control of my mind. I think I may have left my body.

I felt like I was in outer space and at one with the universe. I seemed to understand the reason for everything. I began to hear a voice seeming to come from out in the universe, as I was floating through it. If I were a religious person, I would have believed it was the voice of God. The voice kept telling me to "Come over to the other side." I felt like I would die, if I gave in to the voice. I became frightened because my mind was totally out of my control. Billi was pissed off at my condition. She helped me go to the bedroom and crawl into bed, where I remained until the next morning. Needless to say, our friends went to Victoria's for dinner without us.

When I woke up, I realized that I had been through the greatest hallucinogenic experience of my life. It confirmed to me that the mind is capable of much more than what we use it for in our everyday lives. It is impossible to describe in words all that I experienced under the influence of peyote. Did I actually communicate with some power in the universe or was it all solely created by my own mind as I was hallucinating? Either way, I am convinced that we use only a small fraction of what the mind is ultimately capable of doing. I think I experienced what many other people have experienced down through the ages when they reported religious or near-death experiences and other hallucinations.

What the peyote experience taught me was that if you try this type of hallucinogen, it should be done under the supervision of someone who knows what they are doing. I tried LSD only once and it was a very similar experience, only much more psychedelic and luminous. Material objects came to life and colors took on otherworldly forms and brilliance. I gained great respect for LSD and peyote. They are not to be messed with lightly. But it must be said that hallucinations have inspired many great writers of the past, including Thomas De Quincey, Samuel Coleridge, and Aldous Huxley. Lewis Carroll is believed to have written *Alice in Wonderland* after experiencing natural hallucinations due to migraine headaches. John Lennon and Paul McCartney may never have written "Lucy In The Sky With Diamonds" (LSD) and the *Sgt. Pepper's Lonely Hearts Club Band* album, without one of them experiencing an LSD trip. When it comes to hallucinogens, I do not regret either experience and was grateful for both. I would equate never having had a hallucinogenic experience to never having experienced an orgasm. To describe the feeling of a hallucinogenic experience in words would be as futile as trying to describe the feeling of an orgasm. You have to experience it. By the way, a marijuana-influenced orgasm can be mind-blowing.

I believe that hallucination is where great ideas can come from. Hallucination is a huge leap into the unknown reaches of the mind. You must act on the hallucination, grow mentally from it, however, and then execute the idea you learned from the experience. Hallucination has taught me to think outside of the box. Anyone who has ever done LSD would immediately understand how the Beatles came up with the concept for the *Sgt. Pepper's* album. They translated the LSD experience into music and graphics, and helped to introduce the psychedelic era of the 1960s to the world. In a milder way, marijuana expands my mind, enhances my awareness, and stimulates my creative juices. It makes me look at things from a new perspective.

To paraphrase Steve Jobs, the Apple genius: If Bill Gates did just one LSD trip, Windows would be a better operating system. Jobs used LSD from 1972 through 1974 and said it was a positive, life-changing experience for him. He said LSD was one of the "two or three most important things" he ever did in his life. LSD opened his mind and enabled him to see the world in a different light. He smoked marijuana and hashish and ate pot brownies. He said it helped him relax and made him more creative. I relate to everything he said from my experience with the drugs.

But, like my peyote experience, marijuana can also deliver a negative and paranoid trip. One weekend in 2005 Billi and I went to Newport, Rhode Island, to visit our good friend Peter Hill. When we got there, Peter, who rarely used marijuana, said he had some "great grass." I volunteered to bake some cookies with the weed. I baked the cookies, using the same proportions of marijuana that I used with previous batches of my own less-powerful grass years before. Peter's friend Linda, who is also a friend of ours, was there. She was an experienced marijuana user. She and I ate a whole cookie each. I also ate some crumbs.

We all got into my car to drive the few blocks to a restaurant on the harbor for dinner. As soon as I got in the car, I said, "Man, this is really good weed." We got to the restaurant and as I sat at the table, after ordering a baked stuffed lobster, I looked over toward the bar. I noticed that all the patrons sitting there had very long reptilian tails and lizardlike heads. It was right out of the bar scene in *Star Wars*.

The next thing I knew, I was lying flat on my back under the table, looking up at a bunch of people looking down at me. I took the "backup cookie," which was wrapped in foil, from my pocket and pressed it under the table base, thinking the police might come. Linda, who is about half my size, was pointing at me while laughing her ass off. She ate as much cookie as I did and I heard her say, "He's dead."

This was a big lesson about potency and experience with powerful marijuana. Someone had called a medical unit, which arrived. I walked out to the EMT medical truck. They checked me out and said that they should take me to the hospital because my heart was out of rhythm. I told them I would take myself to the hospital and signed a release stating the same. Timmy, a friend of Peter's who happened to be at the restaurant, drove me to the hospital. Billi, Peter, and Linda followed in another car. When we arrived at the hospital, they checked me out and immediately admitted me.

A doctor came into the room. I told him I ate some marijuana. He checked me out and said I would have to stay overnight or longer, until they got my heart back in the proper rhythm. Luckily the doctor was a heart specialist. I woke up the next morning, a Saturday, and the doctor told me I was greatly improved, but he wanted me to stay one more night. On Sunday, the doctor said my heart was back to normal. He would release me if I promised to come to his office on Monday morning and take some stress tests. I showed up Monday morning, passed the tests and thanked the doctor for all his help. I left Newport with a lot more respect for the potency of the marijuana.

I had consumed too much marijuana of a potency I never before experienced. I hadn't done grass for quite a few years before this incident and didn't realize how potent marijuana had become. This is another reason why marijuana should be legalized and standardized, so that people can avoid negative episodes with the drug. Medical marijuana stores are a big step in this direction. No one wants to experience the hallucinating episode and heart problem that I did. I don't regret having done it because, fortunately, it turned out alright and I learned a great lesson. Since then, I have devised my own system of how much marijuana I can safely ingest after figuring out the potency.

I can't recall ever reading or hearing about someone dying from using marijuana. I do hear about many instances of people dying from abusing alcohol or getting cancer and dying from smoking cigarettes. If the marijuana is eaten, that eliminates the issue of any health problems from smoking it. I do concede that someone could be killed in an automobile accident from a driver consuming too much marijuana. Because of the Newport incident and another, which I will describe next, I never drive after eating marijuana. I limit its use to the privacy of my own home, even though I am now in control of the marijuana I consume because I know its potency.

A few years ago Billi and I drove to Stowe, Vermont, to attend an art opening. When we got there, I ate a marijuana cookie. I knew the potency, and when we left the art gallery about an hour and a half later, the cookie had really kicked in, but I felt it was safe to drive. We were in our sports car with the top down. As we were leaving Stowe, I saw a bunch of blinking police car lights up ahead. I slowly passed the police cars and approached four state troopers standing in a line on my left. The first three troopers waved me ahead and the fourth waved me to a stop. He looked down at me and asked if I had anything to drink. I did not have anything to drink and told him so. Then he asked, "Is there any reason why you don't have your seat belt fastened?" I told him we had just gotten in the car and I hadn't latched it yet. He told me to fasten my seat belt and have a nice evening. Even though I felt safe to drive, I decided to not drive anymore after ingesting marijuana. I lucked out of that one because they were looking for people drinking and driving. I was not impaired, but if they had a test to check for marijuana, it could have ended differently.

When I broke four ribs in 2012, the doctor prescribed oxycodone and hydrocodone for my pain. I don't like taking pills, and they did nothing for my pain. I don't know what all the shouting is about with them. Marijuana, however, is much more pleasant and did help relieve my pain. It also helps manage my pain from arthritis.

I think we have only scratched the surface of the medical benefits of marijuana. Here is a plant you could grow yourself in your garden, costing almost nothing, which could benefit you in many ways. It could eliminate the need for taking a lot of the prescription drugs we are bombarded with in television ads to treat depression, pain, and many other health problems. The side effects of these prescription drugs are myriad and many are more harmful to your health than the original problem you are taking them to treat. Some of the disclaimers even tell you that you could die from taking the medication. Many people actually do die from the side effects or an overdose. As I reported in chapter 1, prescription opioid painkillers like Percocet, Vicodin, OxyContin, and many others are responsible for more overdose deaths than heroin and cocaine combined. In 2013 around 23,000 people died from painkiller and tranquilizer overdoses, and in 2015, 45,000 people died from drug overdoses in the United States.

No matter how many times you experience the joys and possible hallucinations of marijuana, it is impossible to put into words what you felt and experienced afterward. To describe the feeling is truly "beyond words." M.C. Escher, the great graphic artist, said, "If only you knew how entrancing, how stirringly beautiful the images in my head are, the ones I am unable to express." Even though Escher claimed he did not do drugs ("I don't do drugs, my dreams are frightening enough"), his words describe how I feel under the influence of marijuana. Even though it is beyond words, I will attempt to convey to you some of my observations:

I feel totally in the moment, to the point of almost being able to stop time. I believe that is what happened to me back in 1971 in Miami when I seemed to be hanging on the doorknob for a period of time after consuming some powerful marijuana. I begin to sense the understanding of everything because every little thing is magnified. I give myself to it. Everything is alright. I'm experiencing everything in a truly three-dimensional way. I feel that I and everything else, all materialism, is floating weightlessly in the universe, which I believe it really is. I experience the true reality; I am at one with everything around me. My consciousness is greatly expanded. I just know and understand everything better. Everything becomes alive and radiant. I fully appreciate the smallest things and life-forms. Food and drink tastes even better. Marijuana brings a dimension to my mind that can't be accessed without it.

I believe that marijuana can help me understand and feel that there is a way for my mind to perceive another reality, beyond the day-to-day reality that I am conditioned to live in. Marijuana seems to act like a mind cleanser, opening my mind to perceive this alternate reality. If you fully realize and think about the miracle and potential of the human brain, wouldn't an alternate way of perceiving reality be at least a possibility? With marijuana, my mind sometimes shifts gears from day-to-day reality and allows me to perceive a non-human perception of universal truth. I believe that this is what is happening to an even greater degree when a human being is hallucinating.

I have experienced this at times and could actually feel what I thought was the difference between the two realities. I believe that I could find a way to understand more of this alternate reality, but it involves crossing the line into hallucination, which can be a very scary place. After my peyote trip, I prefer to not cross the line.

The thought of crossing the line into an alternate reality, as a student of the universe, is as uncomfortable as a believer trying to give up religion. Neither wants to leave their easy, safe, and comfortable day-to-day reality and belief system.

Sometimes when I write under the influence of marijuana, I can see and feel the notes and words floating on the page, as if I have tapped into the energy of the world around me. I can definitely feel another dimension. I can feel the words and ideas spiraling from my mind and flowing out of the pen. The print is dancing on the page. The pad I write on is floating in space, even though the pad is touching my knee. Time slows; my breathing slows. Marijuana is a consciousness expander. I believe it is where the wisdom is.

I have experienced a morphine (opiate) drip in the hospital. I think of the marijuana experience as a milder and safer form of an opium experience without the addiction problems. Opiates and opioids are some of today's most used and abused prescription drugs for treatment of pain and depression. Opiates are any of the narcotic opioid alkaloids, found as natural products in the opium poppy plant, like morphine and heroin. Opioids are synthetic versions of opiates, and are any chemical that resembles morphine or other opiates in its pharmacological effects. The words opiate and opioid are often used interchangeably, but incorrectly. Opioids work by binding to opioid receptors, which are found principally in the central and peripheral nervous system and the gastrointestinal tract. Marijuana and opioids stimulate a common receptor in the brain's reward pathways. Some opioids include oxycodone, hydrocodone, and fentanyl.

If they received the prescription from a doctor, opioid prescription addicts are like legal heroin addicts. If the addict purchased the prescription drug on the street, he or she will possibly switch to heroin because it is cheaper and more widely available.

From my experience I feel that society would be much better off consuming marijuana than opiates, opioids or alcohol, regardless of the reason people are consuming it. By my observation, it seems to me that the brain works better on marijuana than it does on alcohol. It should be used instead of alcohol, not in addition to alcohol. The user, under the influence of alcohol, eventually could get antagonistic if enough alcohol is consumed and maybe even violent. The user, under the influence of marijuana, will be content, happy, and at peace with everyone and everything. The marijuana user can be much like a dog which rolls over on its back and exposes its belly to the universe.

Thomas De Quincey, in his book "Confessions of an English Opium Eater," published in 1821, made his case against alcohol and in favor of opium in the following quote:

"Crude opium, I affirm peremptorily, is incapable of producing any state of body at all resembling that which is produced by alcohol; and not in degree only incapable, but even in kind; it is not in quantity of its effects merely, but in the quality, that it differs altogether. The pleasure given by wine is always mounting, and tending to a crisis, after which it declines; that from opium, when once generated, is stationary for eight to ten hours: The first, to borrow a technical distinction from medicine is a case of the acute, the second of chronic, pleasure; the one is a flame, the other a steady and equable glow. But the main distinction lies in this, that whereas wine disorders the mental faculties, opium, on the contrary (if taken in a proper manner) introduces among them the most exquisite order, legislation and harmony. Wine robs a man of his self-possession; opium greatly invigorates it."

Unfortunately, opium and its category of opioid drugs have their own set of serious problems: possible overdose, addiction, negative hallucination, and death.

If you substitute the word *marijuana* for *opium* in this statement from Thomas De Quincey, he really nailed it. I could not state a better case for marijuana use instead of alcohol and opioid use. I believe that marijuana is a safer and milder version of opium. If you ingest marijuana, like opium, it will stay in your body and last for up to eight or more hours, even after experiencing the highest point after the first hour to about four hours. The wives of ship captains and sailors on Nantucket in the whaling years (1800s) would use laudanum (a tincture of opium) daily to get them through the long years of waiting for their husbands to return from a sea voyage. I equate this to some men, women, and teenagers who now use prescription drugs (prescribed, purchased on the street, or stolen) to get them through the problems of the day or their life.

I suggest that anyone who needs the crutch of prescription opioid drugs to get them through the day or night or to reduce pain would be much better off if they ingested a controlled amount of marijuana instead. This would eliminate the possibility of an overdose, addiction, or death.

Eating marijuana delivers to me similar effects of opium, though milder, safer, and non-addictive. If you choose to ingest marijuana, never mix drinking alcohol at the same time. If you do, it will almost always lead to a negative experience.

But, and I really mean but… you must treat marijuana with great respect and caution. If you wish to use it, you must educate yourself so you understand what a safe regimen is for you.

18

ANIMATRONICS

In 1981, I went to Hollywood with my friend Seymour Holtzman. He was starting a small chain of animatronic entertainment restaurants similar to Chuck E. Cheese. Seymour asked me to write songs for the animatronic shows. I recorded the songs at Philo Recording Studio in Vermont. We programed the shows in Hollywood. Seymour's restaurant chain was called Circus Playhouse.

That same year I recorded an album of my songs for Earth Audio Records, the record label of Philo. I flew four string players from the Boston Pops orchestra to Vermont for the sessions. I also flew in my favorite rhythm section musician friends from New York City. I overdubbed the strings four times so that they sounded like a full string section. The album was titled *Love Ballet*.

Jon Appleton and Sidney Alonso, two professors at Dartmouth College, invented the Synclavier, a powerful state-of-the-art music synthesizer, or synth. I hired Brad Naples, the president of New England Digital Corporation, to play the Synclavier on my album. The instrument was so new that I was one of the first musicians to record with it. The synth broke down on the first night we used it, but on the second night we were able to get what we wanted. The Synclavier became hugely successful at that time, but it was pricey. It cost from $75,000 to $350,000. Michael Jackson bought three of the most expensive ones for his recording sessions and tours. The high cost became its downfall. Other types of powerful synths became available for around $2,000, so the Synclavier eventually went out of business.

In 1983 I decided to build my own recording studio to record Seymour's animatronic shows and any other work I might get. I converted the three-car garage underneath the 1978 addition to our house into a state-of-the-art recording studio.

While I was building the studio, Synclavier had a convention for users at its manufacturing plant in White River Junction, Vermont. I invited Synclavier to bring all the users to our house for cocktails, followed by a dinner at our restaurant, Victoria's. The great jazz pianist Oscar Peterson and Alby Galuten, the producer of all the Bee Gees' hits, came to the house. When Alby saw the recording studio I was building, he told me, "Your control room is too small." He was totally correct, and two years later I had to break through a concrete wall to accommodate all my synthesizers and extra equipment.

After a year or two, Seymour's board of directors decided they did not want to be in the restaurant business anymore. So there I was, sitting with an expensive recording studio and no work—but not for long.

I was the receiver of a lucky break. In 1986, I read an article in the local paper about an animatronic company, Advanced Animations, which was relocating from Connecticut to Vermont. I immediately got on the phone and called the owner of the company, Bobby Marquis. After I told him I wrote and produced songs for animatronic shows, he invited me to come right over to his house. I found out that Advanced Animations was second only to Disney in the animatronic manufacturing business. Bobby was moving his company because he wanted to live in Vermont. I told him about my experience and played him a bunch of songs. That sealed the deal. I became the producer for most of the music for his animatronic projects.

A week or two later Bobby called me and said he was very frustrated and would be moving back to Connecticut. He had been waiting over a month to have his new factory inspected so he could open his business and he couldn't wait any longer. I told Bobby to stay near the phone. I immediately called my friend Madeleine Kunin, the governor of Vermont, at her home. She said she was leaving for the airport for a trip to Japan to drum up some business for Vermont. I told her there was a guy trying to open his business with fifty employees in Vermont and he couldn't get an inspector to his factory so that he could open. She asked for Bobby's phone number.

Later, Bobby told me he was up on a ladder when the governor called and he thought it was someone playing a joke. Madeleine told Bobby she would have an inspector at his business the following Monday morning, but everything would have to be in order for him to pass the inspection. On Monday, the inspector showed up and Bobby was open for business.

For the next fifteen years, I did just about all the music and sound effects for Bobby and Advanced Animations. Bobby and I grew to become great friends. One Sunday morning, Billi and I were naked in bed, when we were awakened by the Vietnam-like sound of a helicopter crazily blowing and pinning down the shrubs in front of the bedroom window to the ground. We looked out the window and there was Bobby, hovering a few feet off the ground in his helicopter and laughing his ass off, as we frantically tried to cover ourselves. He landed the copter on the ground and came in for a cup of coffee. That was his style.

One of the first animatronic jobs I did for Bobby Marquis was for FAO Schwarz, the high-end toy store on Fifth Avenue in Manhattan. Advanced Animations was building a thirty-foot-tall animated clock tower for their new 80,000-square-foot flagship store. Bobby asked me to write a song to bring the clock tower to life.

I went to the piano and wrote "Welcome to Our World of Toys" in less than an hour:

Welcome to Our World of Toys

Hear the clock tick tock while the children play
Let the fun and laughter chase all cares away
It's a time for joy for all the girls and boys
Welcome to our world of toys
Welcome to our world, welcome to our world
Welcome to our world of toys
Welcome to our world, welcome to our world
Welcome to our world of toys.

I made a simple demo cassette of the song with my daughter Kristina and I singing it and I playing the piano accompaniment. Bobby and I flew to New York to play the song for the president of FAO Schwarz, Peter Harris. We sat in Peter's office and when I hit play on the boom box, Peter got a big smile on his face. "Rewind the tape," he said. When I did, he grabbed the boom box and proceeded to dance through the offices while the boom box blared out the song. I turned to Bobby and said, "I think we just sold him the song!"

I had a $10,000 budget to record it and spent just about all of it for engineers, musicians, and singers to produce the song in my studio. It took over 100 hours of work, but the end result was well worth it.

Bobby Marquis and his family, Billi, Kristina, Erik, and I went to New York for the private grand opening of the store and introduction of the clock tower. It was a beautiful night. As we arrived in a friend's limo, we could hear my clock song reverberating off the nearby skyscrapers and the Plaza Hotel across the street. Spotlights were shining up in the sky, and Kristina's lead singing voice was soaring above the square. It was a huge thrill for all of us.

I suggested FAO sell cassettes of the song in the stores. From the first store on Fifth Avenue, the chain grew to forty-two stores around the country, many with smaller clock towers. The employees were going nuts listening to the song all day long, day after day. Whenever I walked into a store, I never revealed that I wrote the song because I was afraid the employees would kill me.

The clock tower cost $350,000. They eventually sold 100,000 cassettes at five dollars each, which more than paid for the clock. I made royalties on the cassette sales. The song was used in the movie *Big*, starring Tom Hanks, and in Woody Allen's movie *Mighty Aphrodite*. I received licensing fees from both movies. I retained full ownership of the publishing rights to the song, which went on to become a children's classic.

Years later in 1994, I got a call from a New York ad agency. They wanted to use "Welcome to Our World of Toys" in a Christmas television commercial for VISA, the credit card company. They had already filmed the clock for the commercial, but discovered from FAO Schwarz that they couldn't use the song without my permission and paying me a licensing fee. Anyone can record a song after the first usage or recording, as long as they request a license and pay the standard federal copyright royalty per copy sold to the publisher of the song.

However, to use a song in a movie, TV show, or commercial, a licensing fee must be negotiated between the user and the publishing company. I asked for $25,000 to use "Welcome to Our World of Toys" in the VISA commercial for a thirteen-week cycle. This was a very reasonable fee for a well-known song.

They turned down my offer, so I reduced the fee considerably. They turned me down again, saying there was no money left in the advertising budget. I told the guy, "If you're going to spend hundreds of thousands of dollars for each thirty-second spot on network TV and can't pay me a paltry licensing fee to use my song, then don't use it."

Ten minutes after we hung up, I got a call from my contact at FAO Schwarz. He was very angry about the situation, and said FAO wanted to buy the rights to the song. I said I would think about it. The VISA commercial was shown at Christmas, with the clock tower visible, but without my song.

Another reason FAO wanted to buy the song was ASCAP, my music licensing organization. If you have more than two speakers in a store or restaurant or bar, then you must pay ASCAP, BMI, and SESAC if you play any of their music. My song was the only song being played in the store, but ASCAP was hounding FAO to pay a fee of about $1,000 per year per store to use my song. Even though it was only my song being played, the fee would have gone into the whole ASCAP pot, and I would have received almost none of it. But with forty-two stores, FAO would have had to pay serious money.

A few months later I offered to sell FAO Schwarz the ownership of the song for $50,000, which they accepted. I initially thought I didn't charge enough for the song, but as the years went by, I realized that I made a good deal. FAO Schwarz was bought by a Dutch company and eventually went bankrupt. They closed forty stores and only kept open the New York and Las Vegas stores. In 2009, Toys"R"Us bought the two remaining stores and the name. The Las Vegas store eventually closed. The flagship Fifth Avenue store, the last one remaining, closed in July 2015. Toys"R"Us said they were looking for a cheaper location. The stores are gone, but the song remains a children's classic, floating in the frequency waves of the universe. Who knows where it will end up next?

After "Welcome to Our World of Toys," I went on to produce and write many songs for Advanced Animations. The projects, with their hundreds of songs, filled four drawers of a large filing cabinet. The bowling company Brunswick decided to also copy the Chucky Cheese pizza restaurant concept and hired Advanced Animations to build eight large animatronic shows with a circus theme called "Circus World." I wrote twenty-seven songs to bring the circus animal characters to life.

Stew Leonard's, a small chain of supermarkets in Connecticut and New York, uses animatronic characters to entertain shoppers in their stores. I wrote songs for many of their animatronic shows, including the singing milk cartons, "The Farm Fresh Five."

I produced scripts for talking sculptures in an amusement park in Hong Kong. I had to record the dialogue in Mandarin, Cantonese, and English. I hired the head of the Asian studies department at Dartmouth College to find Mandarin and Cantonese speakers, who sat in my recording studio to make sure the actors were saying the correct words. In order to do the Hong Kong job, I had to convert my analog tape studio to digital. The job paid $30,000 and I had to invest $10,000 to buy a computer and Pro Tools software. This allowed me to have complete control in labeling and monitoring the three languages, and assured accuracy in editing the Mandarin and Cantonese, which I, of course, did not understand. We would send weekly recordings to Hong Kong for approval. We never had an error and the job came off without a hitch.

Bobby Marquis was the most creative person I ever worked with. He could build anything from a twenty-six-foot-high dragon, which popped out of a Las Vegas stage spewing forty feet of fire from its mouth, to a waterlog flume ride. He eventually sold Advanced Animations to a Detroit company, which made automotive displays for automobile shows. Bobby and his wife Nancy are still our dear friends.

When I first got into the songwriting business, I would never have imagined that a nice chunk of my income would come from writing songs for singing clock towers, milk cartons, and circus animals. Besides the money, I enjoyed writing the songs to make people happy, especially children.

Left to right: Kristina, Bobby, and Erik. FAO Schwarz Singing Clock, 1986.

19

BILLI, ME, AND POLITICS

Billi always sees the glass half full while I always see it half empty. Billi thinks you can change the world and politics for the better. I am less enthusiastic concerning that model. Billi is an agnostic and I am an atheist. Billi doesn't do marijuana and I love it. Billi likes to be on all kinds of boards, while I'm from the Groucho Marx school of belonging to an organization. I don't want to be a member of any organization that would have me as a member. Billi loves to ski, snowboard, and snowshoe. I hate the cold and don't want to break my leg. Billi loves to run and exercise, while I agree with Mark Twain. If I am going to exert that much energy, I want to accomplish something.

Billi wants to clean out every closet. I want to keep everything because you never know when you are going to need it. Billi would travel anywhere at the drop of a hat. At this stage of my life, I would be happy to never board another airplane. She would probably book a trip on a rocket ship to the moon if we could afford it. I would worry that the rocket ship would blow up in the launch, and if it did take off, we'd probably get lost in some magnetic field or time-warp or something. I would rather spend the money on a Rolls Royce.

Billi is very well organized and immediately tackles whatever has to be done. I am a procrastinator. Don't do today what you can put off until tomorrow. Billi absolutely loves politics. I absolutely abhor politics. Billi contributes to political candidates, whom she thinks will vote according to her political vision. I see it as why would I give money to someone to help them get a job? To me, this is the main reason for what is wrong with the system. The money is given in return for some kind of influence. That is why the rich get richer and the poor get poorer, especially on the national level. Billi is an optimist. I am a pessimist. When we need an item, Billi will buy one. I tend to stock up on it, especially if it is a good buy. Billi wears a seatbelt and I don't. Billi makes assumptions. I never assume anything.

By now, you may ask, how in hell did these two people manage to stay together (happily, I believe) since 1957? Besides a physical law of the universe that opposites attract, we have allowed each other to grow into who we are today–two totally different people from when we met. To put it simply, we love each other and enjoy being together. I think we work together as one person with varied interests. We share everything and make all important decisions together. We share the workload to maintain our homes and lifestyle.

Food-wise, Billi and I are the perfect pair. We both love great food, and she is an excellent cook. I am fortunate to live with an in-house chef. She cooks and I wash the dishes. We both gave up eating meat over forty years ago for spiritual and health reasons, but we eat almost anything else. Billi loves cheese and I don't eat it for health reasons. I can order something with cheese and she will eat the cheese. We have a symbiotic relationship in such matters. If I don't eat the bread crust, she will eat it. Nothing goes to waste.

Aside from my six months in the army in 1959, and trips of a few weeks at a time with Paul Anka in the late sixties, Billi and I have rarely been away from each other for more than a day.

When we lived in Manhattan in the sixties and seventies, Billi couldn't understand why her friend, who lived down the hall in our apartment building, volunteered to work on political campaigns. In NYC the political machine is huge and she felt that volunteering wouldn't be satisfying. At that time, she was slowly emerging from her Republican upbringing and becoming an Independent voter.

Then we moved to Vermont where political activity felt much more personal and candidates were very accessible to their constituents. In early 1980 Billi attended a day-long seminar sponsored by Planned Parenthood. The focus was to train volunteers how to become politically active and be part of the newly-formed Friends of Planned Parenthood. She learned that a handful of phone calls to your state representative on a certain issue really could make a difference.

She was very concerned that the conservatives in the legislature wanted to cut all public funding to Planned Parenthood of Vermont because they referred women who needed abortions to out-of-state clinics. No such procedures were performed in Vermont. A large cut in funding would have been a tragedy, since the Vermont chapter was recognized nationally as one of the most effective providers of rural health care for women.

After that fateful seminar, Billi started getting involved in the Vermont Democratic Party and the Vermont Women's Political Caucus. There was no turning back. She had found her mission. She loved the organizing, the persuading, and the deep involvement in the issues of the day.

While I dislike politics, I've joined Billi for the ride. She handles the politics and I handle the music, which she has always fully supported. That same year, I did a benefit concert for the local Chandler Center for the Arts, and Madeleine Kunin, who was the Lieutenant Governor of Vermont at the time, attended. After the concert, I invited all the musicians, some friends, and Madeleine to our house for a party. People were all over the house, and at one point, I noticed a clean-cut, good-looking guy in a suit and tie, obviously not a musician, standing at ease in one corner of the dining room. I asked Billi who he was, and she said, "He's a state trooper guarding Madeleine, who is acting governor today because the governor is out of state."

I immediately panicked and ran upstairs to my library office. Some of the musicians were inside and others were out on the balcony, smoking pot. I told them there was a state cop in the house and to put out the joints, open the windows, and air themselves out thoroughly before coming downstairs. To this day, I don't know whether the state trooper or Madeleine had any idea of what was going on upstairs.

In 1982 I organized a three-concert tour of Vermont with twenty-seven musicians to raise money for Madeleine when she ran for governor the first time. The tour was a bust because of lousy publicity, and Madeleine lost the election. Two years later, she ran again and became the first female governor in the history of Vermont. She was elected for a total of three terms.

After being an elementary school teacher for ten years in Pennsylvania and New York City, Billi spent the next seventeen years as a full-time mother and homemaker. During that time, we moved from Manhattan to Vermont with our two children, Erik and Kristina.

When our children were teenagers, Billi was employed as the director of development for the Vermont Institute of Natural Science in Woodstock, having served previously as vice-president of the board of trustees. She held that position for sixteen years.

Since 1980, she has been actively involved in the struggle for women's rights, serving as vice president of the National Women's Political Caucus, chair of the Vermont Women's Political Caucus, and chair of the Vermont Governor's Commission on Women. She was the founding chair of the Vermont Women's Fund, which now has an endowment of over two million dollars. In 2005 she received the first Classic Woman Award from *Traditional Home* magazine for her work establishing the Vermont Women's Fund.

In 1999 Billi received the first David W. Curtis Leadership Award for her fundraising activities on behalf of the Vermont Democratic Party. She has been a delegate to six Democratic National Conventions. In 2000 she was chair of the Vermont delegation to the Democratic National Convention. In 2008 she served on the Rules Committee of the convention, and served on the Credentials Committee in 2012.

At the 2004 Vermont Democratic State Convention she was elected Democratic National Committeewoman. She was re-elected in 2008 and 2012. She has been elected to three terms on the Credentials Committee of the DNC. Billi also served on the Board of Directors of Blue Cross Blue Shield of Vermont for sixteen years. In 2001 she organized the Vermont Committee of the National Museum of Women in the Arts. She served as its president for five years.

Currently, Billi serves on the boards of Burlington City Arts, the Brookfield Community Partnership, and the Vermont Democratic Party. She is the principal of BG Consulting, providing development advice for nonprofit organizations.

If you think that this sounds like one hell of a resume, you would be correct. I am proud of Billi's accomplishments and must confess that I had some fun along the way. I especially enjoyed eating for free at the parties during the Democratic National Conventions.

I consider myself an independent and joke about Billi being a knee-jerk Democrat. So, how did we end up in the White House on the day that Ronald Reagan returned from the hospital after the assassination attempt on March 30, 1981? Our Republican friends Evie and Seymour Holtzman were friends with Helene Von Damm. She was Reagan's secretary when he was governor of California and when he first became president.

Later, Reagan appointed her Deputy Director of Presidential Personal in the White House. She finally was appointed ambassador to Austria, where she was born.

Around 1979 the Holtzmans brought Helene to ski and stay with Billi and me in Vermont. She stayed with us a few times more, whenever she wanted to ski in Vermont. Helene, Billi, and I hit it off immediately. Politics didn't matter at all. We just enjoyed hanging out together.

In early 1981 Helene invited Evie and Seymour and Billi and me to the White House for a weekend in April. Meanwhile John Hinckley made his assassination attempt on March 30. On Saturday, April 11, we all had lunch in the White House mess. After lunch Helene showed us the Oval Office. Then she had us wait in the ante-room with Vice President George Bush, his wife, Barbara, and members of the cabinet and their wives. A short time later, Helene took all of us out to the White House lawn. Within minutes, the presidential helicopter landed right in front of us. Reagan was returning from the hospital where he was recovering from Hinckley's attack. The small crowd of welcomers applauded as Nancy and Ron disembarked. Even though Billi and I were probably the only non-Republicans there, it was a touching historical moment.

That night Helene took us to a small private room in the Kennedy Center for the Performing Arts. It was a very comfortable space with red velvet walls and the presidential seal above the small bar. The bartender made any drink you wanted while the waiter passed artful and tasty hors d'oeuvres. Besides the waiter and bartender, Helene and her husband, Byron, Evie, Seymour, Billi, and I were the only ones in the room.

A few minutes before 8:00 P.M., the waiter flung open the large double doors. We all realized that Helene was leading us into the Presidential Box. As we sat down, all eyes in the hall seemed to be on us. The audience was trying to figure out who the hell we were.

We enjoyed the play, which was "The Little Foxes," starring Elizabeth Taylor. After the show, Helene said, "I have one more surprise for you." She led us through a maze of hallways to the back stage and knocked on a door. The door opened and there was Elizabeth Taylor in her dressing room. She knew Helene because her husband at that time was Senator John Warner of Virginia. She had on her full stage make-up and was drinking whiskey. She offered us a drink. She was cordial and very charming, and gave us her full attention during our visit.

The weekend was a surreal and memorable experience for an Independent and a Democrat from Vermont who both were at odds with basically everything Reagan stood for. Billi and I were very impressed with the weekend Helene lavished on us. We thoroughly enjoyed it and appreciated her kindness. The last time we spoke with Helene she said she was "disgusted with the Republican party" because of the dramatic shift to the radical right.

One morning in 1984 at 6:00 A.M. the phone rang. I reached for it on my side of the bed and a male voice asked, "Is Billi there?" I responded, "Who is this?" The voice answered, "Howard Dean." I asked, "Howard who?" and handed the phone to Billi. When she hung up, I asked, "What the hell was that about?"

She said Howard, who was running for lieutenant governor, called to tell her that presidential candidate Walter Mondale just announced that Geraldine Ferraro was his running mate for vice president. Billi and Howard were both elated because they had been travelling around Vermont speaking to groups about why it was time for a female candidate for vice president.

At that time, I was spearheading a campaign to run some guys out of town for trying to build a woodchip plant in Randolph, Vermont. Their idea was to burn 900 tons of woodchips a day with a 200-foot-high smokestack and generate electricity for the sole purpose of selling the electricity back to the grid, under the terms of the Purpa Law. They were a group of opportunists from Florida who called themselves the Decker Organization. We called ourselves DOA for dead on arrival and Decker Opposition Association.

Decker proposed running fifty forty-foot trailer truckloads of woodchips a day through Randolph to supply the plant. The trucks would run by our restaurant, Victoria's, and over an unsafe bridge while the woodchip plant smokestacks polluted the town. At their initial meeting to inform the public, I stood up and announced that "they would build the plant over my dead body." At the end of Decker's dog and pony show, I stood up again and announced, "Anyone here who opposes this ridiculous idea meet me up front so we can start organizing." Around sixty people signed up that night. Two weeks later, at least 200 people who opposed Decker's plan turned out at Chandler Music Hall for our first meeting. We put up such resistance that after nine weeks and after Decker had spent $350,000, Decker put its tail between its legs, abandoned their project, and quietly left town.

I guess the political bug was catching. I had been trying to recruit politicians to our side and none would join us because if Decker went forward, it would have included about twenty-five low-paying jobs. A few weeks after Howard Dean's early morning phone call to Billi, he called me and asked to speak at a rally we were going to have in the town square. I consented because he was the only politician with the balls to do so. I greatly admired his courage.

Two days before the rally, Decker abandoned their idea and we changed the rally to a victory celebration, which was attended by hundreds of people. This was a great audience for Howard. As a Democrat, he was elected lieutenant governor under Richard Snelling, a Republican. Howard became governor after Snelling died while in office. Billi and I hosted a fundraising dinner for his first campaign for governor, which eighty people attended at our house. He was governor for twelve years. Howard ran for president in 2004. We all know that outcome.

In March 2008 Billi was a fundraiser for Hillary Clinton's first campaign for president. As a reward, Billi was invited to a small private reception for about forty major donors at the Fairmont Copley Plaza in Boston. Bill Clinton spoke and everyone got a photo-op with him. I had tagged along and when our photo-op came up, Billi was on Clinton's right side and I was on his left. Billi and Bill were facing each other in conversation, while the photographer was setting up the shot. Seeing that they were not facing the camera, I said, "Bill, look at the camera." Billi and Bill both snapped around and the photo was taken.

On the drive home to Vermont late that night, I suddenly realized that Clinton thought I was ordering *him* to face the camera—my nickname for Billi is Bill. Now I was mortified. Billi and I laughed so hard that I almost drove off the road.

Back in 1980, Billi helped organize a rally on the Vermont State House lawn to protect women's reproductive rights. Billi held up a sign in front of each speaker limiting their talk to five minutes. Governor Snelling spoke and Billi held up her sign, stating that one minute was left, which Snelling totally ignored. Billi continued to hold the sign up while shaking it. About fifteen minutes later when Snelling got off the podium, he was heard to say, "Who the hell is that woman with the sign?"

Needless to say from that day forward, Billi was not one of Snelling's favorite people. In 1991 Snelling sent Billi a letter thanking her for her service as chair of the Governor's Commission on Women. He wrote that it was time to appoint a new chair. It was a political move that greatly disappointed her. A few days later, Billi and I were in Nantucket when we heard that Snelling had just died. I jokingly told Billi she was lucky we were out of state when he died or she could be investigated as a suspect in his death. He actually died of a heart attack after an early evening swim in his pool. He had not yet appointed a new chair of the Commission, so Howard, as the new governor, kept Billi on the nonpaying job for five more years. She stepped down in 1996.

When Hillary Clinton ran for president in 2008, Billi was a super delegate to the Democratic National Convention and was very active in Hillary's Northeast Campaign Committee. One night around 9:00 the phone rang and I answered it. The voice asked, "Is Billi there?" I said, "Who is this please?" The voice said, "This is Hillary." Hillary knew how to keep in touch with her faithful supporters like Billi. As a super delegate to the DNC, Billi supported Hillary until the second day of the convention, when she released her delegates to vote for Obama.

President Barack Obama and Billi, 2012

President Bill Clinton with Billi and Bobby, 2008

First Lady Hillary Clinton with Billi, 1992

Left to right: Senator Patrick Leahy, Governor Madeleine Kunin,
Vice President Al Gore, Billi, and Bobby, 1994

Hillary and Billi, 2015

Billi and Bobby with the United States Marine Band in the East Room of the White House at a reception hosted by President Barack Obama, 2011

Governor Howard Dean with Billi at a dinner for eighty people at the Gosh residence, 1992

Billi in the library, 2005
Credit: Michael Wechsler

20

NANTUCKET

In 1946 Billi's paternal grandparents purchased a second home in Nantucket, Massachusetts, the island thirty miles out in the ocean from Cape Cod. The house was built in 1750. A Quaker whaling ship captain named Peleg Bunker eventually bought the house, which became known as the Captain Peleg Bunker house.

According to Edouvard A. Stackpole and Melvin B. Summerfield in their 1974 Hasting House book *Nantucket Doorways, Thresholds to the Past*,

Captain Bunker was one of those Nantucket ship-masters who went to Dunkirk with the ship owner William Rotch in 1785; he commanded the whaleships *Hope* and *Ardent* on two successful voyages out of that French port. After the French Revolution had forced the Nantucket colony of whalemen to abandon Dunkirk, Captain Bunker went to London to take command of the former Rotch ship *Falkland*, which had been captured by the British while she sailed under the French flag. Through an ironic twist of fate, the *Falkland* was recaptured in the English Channel by a French privateer, and Captain Bunker and his men were treated barbarously by their captors, being marched from the coast to a prison in Verdun. The year was 1804.

During the next five years all efforts to obtain the release of Captain Bunker were rebuffed by the Napoleonic authorities in France. Finally, in 1809, an agreement was reached and the Nantucket whaleman was released. But his health had been so seriously undermined by his imprisonment that he died before he could reach the coast and embark for home. Back in Nantucket, his widow, Lydia Gardner Bunker, and his seven children were to mourn his passing.

But the tragedy besetting this family did not end here. At the outbreak of the Anglo-French War, Captain Bunker's eldest son, Captain Obed Bunker, while in command of the Rotch ship *Greyhound*, was captured by a Dutch privateer in Delagoa Bay, on the east coast of Africa. Only a few years after Captain Peleg's death in France, his son Captain Tristram Bunker, while on a voyage to the Pacific Ocean as master of the London whaler *Scorpion*, went ashore in a small port on the coast of Chili and was attacked by desperadoes and killed.

Billi's grandparents, Richard and Edna Williams, carefully restored the house, leaving all the historic features intact. The house has seven fireplaces and a roof walk (sometimes called a widow's walk). All the hand-forged hardware is original and intact. The 265-year-old wide pumpkin-pine floorboards and paneled walls are "king's wood," stolen from the king's land in Maine and shipped to Nantucket where there were no trees. The windows, still with original glass, are twelve-over-twelve panes or nine-over-nine.

Billi began visiting the house in 1947 when she was eleven years old. I began visiting the house with Billi around 1965. When Billi's grandfather died in 1977, her Aunt Muriel Williams inherited the house. We visited yearly until Muriel (or Auntie Mue as we called her) died in 2007. Mue left the house to Billi and her brother Bill. Bill had no interest in keeping it and generously and graciously gave his half ownership to Billi to keep it in the family. We are forever grateful to Bill as we both love the house and Nantucket dearly.

Nantucket grows on you, deep into your soul. Many of the historic houses are protected and look much like they did nearly 300 years ago. Walking the streets makes you feel like you are living in the days of whaling, ship captains, and gas lights. Before the tourists come in the summer and after they leave in the fall, Billi and I walk on Main Street and feel as if we are transported back hundreds of years. Some nights we are the only people on the Main Street square, which on a summer day would be filled with thousands of tourists. In moments like this, we feel like it is our own private island. The historic district in downtown Nantucket, where our house is located, is the real deal. This is not a Disneyland recreation. The buildings exist as they did centuries ago. Chain stores are not allowed on Nantucket. The whole island is preserved, protected and controlled. As a result, Nantucket retains its authenticity, charm and beauty.

You can only get to Nantucket by boat or airplane. The ferryboat rides are a charming introduction to what awaits you on the island. Islanders, tourists, workmen, summer residents, student sports teams, children, and dogs are the usual mix of passengers. Permanent residents number around 10,000 and more than 50,000 tourists visit in the summer. When islanders go to the mainland to shop, they say they are going to America.

In 2002, Billi's Aunt Muriel was the second person on Nantucket to preserve a house with an easement with the Nantucket Preservation Trust (NPT). No changes can be made to the walls and main interior features, such as hardware, windows, and fireplaces, in perpetuity. The NPT has called the house, "one of the finest examples of a typical Nantucket house on the island." In 2014 the NPT posthumously gave Aunt Muriel The Stewardship Award for excellence in preservation. From April to December each year, Billi and I alternate two weeks in Nantucket and two weeks in Vermont. We love both places.

The Peleg Bunker house is the perfect place for Billi and me to immerse ourselves in history while we relax and reflect on life. Nantucket stimulates and recharges my creative batteries in much the same manner as marijuana.

21

BJÖRK AND BILL BRYSON

One of the clients in my recording studio was Porter Music Box Company. My son Erik, who was my recording engineer from 1985 to 2004, recorded all of Porter's music box CDs. Porter made very high-end music boxes for an international clientele. In 2001, Björk, the pop singer from Reykjavik, Iceland, commissioned Porter to build a custom music box for her upcoming album and concert tour. The music box played large, perforated metal discs, which were two feet in diameter. The box itself was made of see-through Lucite and stood on four legs. It cost $30,000.

Björk had just starred in Lars Von Trier's movie *Dancer in the Dark*. She won the best female performance award at the 2000 Cannes Film Festival. She was also nominated for an Academy Award; she appeared at the ceremony that year in her famous swan dress.

She needed to record the music box in Vermont in order to meet the deadline for her CD release. Porter suggested my studio to record the music box and sent some samples of the quality of our work to her. Björk booked the studio and flew from London to Vermont for the recording date.

She arrived at the house, accompanied by her engineer, who would oversee the recording, which was engineered by Erik. She was a diminutive figure, wearing curled-toe, elflike shoes. Björk was courteous and warm and I liked her immediately. As soon as we walked into the studio, she went into the vocal booth where the large music box was set up with two Neumann U87 microphones. Neumanns are considered to be among the best mics available. She called for a third mic to be set up under the music box. After a few more adjustments, with her listening in the control room, she said she was ready to record.

While Erik made a final adjustment in the booth, Björk was sitting in the engineer's chair and I overheard her say to her engineer, "I love this place." Now knowing that she was happy with everything, I was able to relax. She was a consummate professional. Erik engineered the session and everything went well.

After the session, we went up into the house, and I opened a bottle of good wine, which Björk enjoyed. We had a nice, long conversation and then I sent her on her way with another bottle of the same wine. The recordings appeared on her *Vespertine* album, which was released a short time later.

Another interesting client in my recording studio was Bill Bryson, who wrote the bestselling book *A Walk in the Woods*, which also became a movie in 2015. In 2004, his publisher wanted him to go to New York City to record the audiobook version of *A Short History of Nearly Everything*. Though his home is in London, he was temporarily living in Hanover, New Hampshire. He told the publisher he did not want to travel to New York to record.

The producer found my studio in a national listing and decided we had the proper equipment to do the job. We were less than an hour's drive from Bill's house. He commuted to my studio for a week. He was a friendly and very funny guy. He had a good rapport with my son Erik, who engineered the project. When the recording was finished, Bill signed the manuscript he was working with and gave it to me as a gift.

Building a recording studio in Vermont was similar to building the baseball field in the movie *Field Of Dreams*. Build it and they will come. I never know who will turn up next.

22

ART STORIES

In 1959, as newlyweds, Billi and I bought a few paintings from a local college student to hang in our apartment in Reading. We thought this was a better idea than buying prints at the local five-and-dime. One was of a clown and one depicted a streetscape. In the early 1960s we purchased an unframed painting of a ballerina dancer that looked like a Degas at a sidewalk art show in New York. I found a gilt frame at an antique store that fit the large painting perfectly. That began our art collection. We now own more than 1,000 works of art. We have two storage rooms for the art that does not fit into the house.

When we moved to Vermont, I would go to country auctions whenever I could to buy antiques for our house. I would occasionally see a painting I liked and I would buy it. One day in the mid-1970s, I parked my car at an auction, and as I walked up a short hill to the tent, I saw the auctioneer hold up a painting and ask for a starting bid of five dollars. As I entered the tent, I could see the painting up close. It was a winter landscape with a group of people standing and skating on the ice in front of a castle-like house, with mountains in the distance. There was something about it that caught my eye. The auctioneer got up to a bid of ten dollars. I bid eleven dollars and won the painting. I took it home and put it in a closet. It was signed "A. Doll, München" and was unframed.

A few years later, in 1979, I saw an ad in the *New York Times* for the Daniel B. Grossman Art Gallery in New York City. It offered up to $30,000 for paintings by a list of German painters. One of the painters listed was Anton Doll. I called the gallery and described the painting. They offered to fly to Vermont to see the painting. I told them I would bring it to New York on my next trip. A few weeks later, I walked into the gallery and the secretary ushered me into a room with a large black velvet easel, where she placed my painting. There were about a half-dozen Anton Doll paintings hanging in the gallery.

Daniel Grossman walked into the room and shook my hand. He was a tall, dignified-looking gentleman, dressed in an expensive suit. He verified that the painting was painted by Anton Doll in Munich, Germany around 1860. Doll was born in 1826 and died in 1887. Grossman shined a black light on the painting and pointed out an area which he said was poorly over-painted and repaired. The painting also needed to be cleaned. He offered me $16,000 for the painting, as is. I immediately figured the painting was worth double that since he had to fix it and make a profit. I told him I would think about it and call him if I decided to sell it.

He said if I left the painting with him, he would have the over-painted spot removed with a solvent to reveal the extent of the damage. He would then send me a transparency of the painting showing the damage. He gave me a receipt for the painting and I left it with him.

A few weeks late, I received the transparency showing a cross-like clean cut a few inches wide. I called Daniel and he said it would cost $2,000 to have the painting cleaned and repaired, and again offered me $16,000. I told him I didn't want to sell and would have my manager pick up the painting. Daniel was disappointed, so I knew it was a desirable work of art, worth at least double his offer on the retail market. Besides, I really liked the painting and was not ready to give it up.

A few years later, I was in our restaurant, Victoria's, when my manager said a guy having lunch wanted to meet me. He admired some of the paintings hanging in the restaurant. I told him I had other paintings at home, including an Anton Doll. His name was Gerald Hoepfner, and he was the head art restorer at the Clark Institute at Williams College in Massachusetts. He was in Vermont to restore some paintings in the Vermont State House in Montpelier. I invited him to the house to see the Anton Doll.

When Gerald saw the painting, he said the cost his laboratory would charge to clean and repair the painting would be $2,000, exactly what Grossman had quoted. However, Gerald said he would clean and repair it himself for $1,000 in his spare time, but it would take about five months. I consented and gave him the painting, which was twenty-four by forty-two inches. About five months later, he returned the painting, which was beautifully cleaned and restored. He relined the canvas and mounted it on a metal museum stretcher. The painting was later appraised for $24,000 to $30,000, according to auction results. Not bad for a $1,011 total investment. I framed the painting and it hangs over our bed to this day. If it were a song, I'd say I scored a top ten hit.

In 1978, while driving in Vermont, I noticed a sign that said Sale Barn. I drove in the long driveway and saw a man painting in the open doorway of the barn. He was working on a large mural, which was painted in the social realist style of the 1930s. He introduced himself as Ron Slayton. He was restoring the painting, which he had painted in the 1930s, for the Fleming Museum in Burlington, Vermont, which owned the painting. I asked if he had any paintings for sale and he showed me various paintings around the barn. He took me up into the attic of his house and showed me a 1930s painting called *Burlington Gothic, Pie In The Sky*, which I instantly loved. It pictured a workman with his lunchbox and his family outside of their tenement house, with smokestacks and iron beams crashing around them. A cornucopia of fruits and vegetables loomed over the family's heads. Ron said the painting was not for sale.

I bought two paintings from Ron that day: *Two Worlds*, a 1942 modern landscape oil painting, and *Vermont Godiva*, a watercolor he recently had painted of a farmer daydreaming in his field by a fence with his broken-down horse. A series of poses of the same naked woman falling off a white horse appeared above his head across the top of the painting. I was hooked. I returned to his barn a few more times and bought more paintings.

Ron often told me stories about his life as a young artist during the Great Depression. He would take vegetables from neighbors' gardens to survive. Sometimes he would go to a diner and order a glass of water. He would then pour the ketchup that was on the table into the water to make a kind of thin tomato soup. When the University of Vermont hired him to rid one of its bell towers from pigeons, he went up, killed them with a baseball bat, and took them home for dinner.

Ron became a painter under Franklin Roosevelt's Works Progress Administration (WPA) program and earned eighteen dollars a week. In 1939 he had a show of his paintings at the University of Vermont. When the show was over he couldn't afford to pick up his paintings. Some found their way onto classroom walls at the university. Many years later some of them ended up in the Fleming Museum. Others, as Ron would often say, "were up for grabs."

A few months after meeting Ron, I invited him and his wife, Mayette, who was also a very good painter, to come to our house for drinks, followed by dinner at our restaurant. Ron appeared at our door with a large package wrapped in brown paper. After some hors d'oeuvres, (Ron and Mayette did not drink), Ron handed the package to me and said it was a gift. In the package was the painting *Burlington Gothic, Pie In The Sky*, which was not for sale when I saw it in his attic. I told him the gift was too generous and I could not accept it. Ron said, "I have a feeling that you are going to be my historian, when I die." I said, "Ron, I am your historian and you can count on it." I loved the painting and did not want to insult Ron, so I accepted it.

We became cherished friends and I looked up to Ron, who was 68 years old at the time, as a kind of respected father image. He was a wonderful humanitarian and a true gentleman. Over the years, I bought many more paintings from Ron and helped him secure shows in quite a few galleries. A major retrospective was presented at the T.W. Wood Gallery, a museum in Montpelier, Vermont, in 1989, three years before he died. In 1990 I commissioned him to do a portrait of our family. It was to be six by four feet, with a portrait of each one of us in each quadrant of the painting. About a year later, Ron asked permission to paint it in four three by two feet panels because his health was failing and he could not reach high any more. I said that would be fine.

About six months later, Ron said the paintings were finished. It was a cold November day when he and I walked slowly from his house to the barn to see the paintings. As Ron walked with his cane, he told me he had leukemia. I was crushed to hear that my friend was dying. When we got to the barn and I saw the beautiful portraits he painted from photographs of our family, my emotions ran away with me and I totally lost it. These were the last paintings Ron ever painted.

He spent the last weeks of his life lying on the couch in his living room. I visited him a few times a week. He had painted two large social realist watercolor murals in 1984. I advised him to donate them to the Fleming Museum, which had about a dozen of his 1930s social realist WPA paintings. By doing this, he could write off the value of them on his taxes for estate reasons. He told me he didn't want the murals hidden in a museum store room and said he was giving them to me as a gift to be shown in public, whenever I could make it possible. I have done just that.

One of the murals was *The Last Supper*, a social realist painting from 1984. It is comprised of ten thirty- inch by twenty-four-inch watercolor panels, for a total mural size of five by ten feet. It is an antiwar protest painting. In the late 1990s I exhibited the mural at the Chandler Gallery in Randolph, Vermont. The painting depicted an army general eating a plate of soldiers as business men and politicians offered him money and munitions, and the voters slept by a burnt candle with cobwebs. The table they were seated at was being held up by poor people acting as table legs.

Chandler Gallery was also used by the town as a polling place. The gallery contacted me and said the town wanted the mural removed, so that it wouldn't be seen by voters and potentially offend them. I asked if they were removing the other paintings in the show. They said, no. I said my polling place in Brookfield was the Masonic temple and I had to look at a copy of the religious painting of *The Last Supper* when I voted and, as an atheist, I was offended. I told the town I wouldn't remove the painting. They backed down and moved the polling place to the music hall next door. I don't believe in censoring the arts.

Ron died in July 1992. He was 81 years old. I loved him and miss him very much. He was a wonderful human being.

In June 2010 the Fleming Museum exhibited "A Centennial Celebration," a retrospective of Ron and Francis Colburn in celebration of the 100th anniversary of both their births. Colburn is another favorite artist of mine, whom we also collect. Ron and Francis were lifelong friends.

In 1987 Betty Stern, wife of my late stockbroker Eddy Stern, called and said she had to sell her M.C. Escher lithograph, which Billi and I often admired at their home. She had dated Cornelius Roosevelt Jr. in the 1950s and he gave it to her as a gift. Roosevelt was an obsessive collector of Escher. When he died, he left his entire collection of Eschers to the National Gallery of Art in Washington, DC.

Betty offered Escher's *House Of Stairs*, signed and numbered 22 to us for the price a dealer had offered her. She said she would rather have us own it, so Billi and I bought it for the wholesale price and have lived with it happily ever after. In the late 1990s, on a visit to the National Gallery of Art, I had the privilege of viewing the entire collection of Eschers in the museum. They ushered me into a private room, supplied me with white gloves, and brought one storage box at a time for my perusal. It was a mind-blowing afternoon.

In the late 1980s I saw a large painting in a shop in Montpelier, Vermont. It showed an older, Native-American woman standing in the raised bucket of a huge front loader, which was building a nuclear plant on an Indian reservation in Arizona. I bought the painting and soon became friends with the artist, Philip Hagopian, whose mother was part Native American and his father was Armenian. Like Ron Slayton, Philip is a social realist painter depicting the injustices of society. He also paints beautiful landscapes. I was especially attracted to his social realist works. Billi and I began to collect his earlier examples, which he painted in his early twenties. After buying the first painting from Philip, I asked him if he had more paintings for sale. He said he had been painting in an old town hall in Plainfield, Vermont, which he was using as a studio, rent free. The owner decided to charge Philip rent retroactively without notifying him. Philip couldn't afford to pay the back rent, which was in arrears by $250. The owner locked the door. Philip could not access his nearly 100 paintings and drawings inside. I advanced Philip the rent and we removed the works from the town hall to Philip's house. I was able to secure a retrospective exhibition for Philip in 1993 at the T.W. Wood Gallery. We now have a large collection of Philip's paintings.

In 1989 we found an artist we liked in a Nantucket gallery. We purchased two carved and painted works and found out that he lived in Vermont. His name was Stephen Huneck, a self-taught carver. I sought him out in Vermont. I loaned him $1,000 the first day I met him and brought collectors to him, who bought a large volume of his work. He made beautiful furniture. Billi and I bought one of his largest pieces, *CEO Sideboard*, which has eighty-nine businessmen carved on it. It was originally an altar in a Catholic church. Huneck carved a large businessman in place of the missing Christ in the center. That was a brilliant move, and consistent with my artistic, atheist, and business philosophy. It was right up my alley and I loved it. The piece was shown in magazines around the world. It was exhibited at the Currier Museum in New Hampshire in a show of fine American furniture.

In 2011 Stephen had to lay off about ten of his assistants due to the lingering recession even though he had become internationally famous over the previous two decades. A few days later, after becoming very depressed, he parked his car in front of his psychiatrist's office and shot himself fatally in the head. In 2013 his wife Gwen died suddenly and the rumor was that she also committed suicide. What a tragedy.

In 1989, I saw an auction listing for the estate sale of a Vermont artist I had never heard of, Jane Farrell. She was a painter and maker of wooden found-object sculptures and was influenced by Louise Nevelson. When I arrived at the auction in Reading, Vermont, I noticed at least seventy black, wooden box sculptures scattered all over the place. I bought them all. I had bought the excellent life's work of this deceased artist for a bargain. There were over 300 people and many of Farrell's relatives at the auction. No one was interested in her work, not even her family.

I hired a friend to pick them up for me in his sixteen-foot trailer, which he filled to the brim. The friend was laughing as we loaded the trailer, thinking I was nuts and had made a huge blunder. I also bought around sixty of her oil paintings for a low price. Later, I had a show of her sculptures in a restaurant and sold the first one for more money than I paid for all the sculptures and paintings combined. After selling a few sculptures and giving some away to friends and Farrell's family, I decided to keep the remainder because I like living with them.

In 1999 while visiting our friend Peter Hill in Newport, Rhode Island, we discovered the artist Tom Deininger. He makes large assemblages from found objects, including plastic action figures, Barbie dolls, and McDonald's plastic toys. I walked into a juried show at a church. About sixty-feet down the aisle, I saw what I thought was a realist painting eight by eight feet in size. It depicted a guy sitting in his yard in a lawn chair. When I got up close, my mind was blown. It was made of thousands of plastic objects, including cut-up garden hoses simulating a lawn. It excited me more than any other modern artwork I had ever seen anywhere. To explain why I love a certain work of art would be as futile as attempting to explain how I feel under the influence of marijuana. It is beyond words and instantly makes me feel good while stimulating my mind.

I pried Tom's phone number from the minister at the church and called him. Billi and I stopped by his studio and made arrangements to buy three of his works: an eight-by-eight-foot assemblage of three sisters standing in a yard, which he had just begun working on; a large black-and-white assemblage of two profiles of a friend; and a small assemblage of another friend. A few months later, Tom delivered the works to our house in Vermont and installed them. We became good friends. About a year later, Tom got married, and Billi and I were invited to a wedding cruise around Newport harbor.

Before that, Tom had a very successful show at the Newport Art Museum. The centerpiece of the show was a twelve-foot-high by twenty-foot-wide mural of a flower-strewn meadow with a tree line and a snow-covered mountain. It reminded Billi and me of the view in front of our Vermont house. Tom had a contract with an art dealer, who represented him not very successfully. Soon after the show, they parted ways. On his wedding weekend, Tom offered the mural, *Plastic Paradise*, to Billi and me for a very enticing price because he needed to make room in his studio. I told Tom, "You'd better ask your wife to approve the deal because you are married now." Tom returned from his honeymoon and said we had a deal. About a year later, we decided to add an entrance room gallery onto my recording studio in order to house the mural and the rest of Tom's work. We call it The Deininger Gallery.

Anyone who comes into the room has their mind blown, just like I did upon seeing Tom's work for the first time. In 2010 our good friends, Marc vanderHeyden, who was president of St. Michael's College until recently, and his wife, Dana, brought an art professor to see Tom's work in our gallery. Later, the art professor while on sabbatical at the Smithsonian American Art Museum in Washington, DC, told the chief curator of the museum, Dr. Eleanor Harvey, about our art collection. Eleanor came to our house to see our collection and asked if she could bring twenty-five members of the Smithsonian's Art Forum to view our collection as part of a tour of art venues in northern New England. The tour would include the Shelburne Museum and the Hood Museum at Dartmouth College. We, of course, agreed and on October 1, 2010, Eleanor and the director Elizabeth "Betsy" Broun, along with twenty-five collectors came to our house. They were all blown away by Tom's assemblages. The chairman of the board of the Smithsonian American Art Museum and his wife commissioned Tom to make two large assemblages for their private collection. The museum expressed serious interest in acquiring *Plastic Paradise* to add to their collection. They later decided the mural was too large. They have been in touch with Tom regarding a possible commission for a smaller work.

Another favorite artist in our collection is the Vermont sculptor John Matusz. Billi and I were looking for some large-scale sculptures to place outdoors. John is a master welder who works with steel and stone and creates wonderful abstract works, from small table pieces to large outdoor works weighing several tons. John also painted large abstract works in the nineteen eighties and continues to draw figuratively when he is not sculpting. We are fortunate to have his work in our collection, and to have him as a cherished friend.

I buy art because I love it. But if it appreciates in value, that's even better. I don't play the stock market, so I depend somewhat on my art to be an investment, or at least retain the value of what I paid for it. When I bought the Anton Doll painting at auction for eleven dollars, neither the seller nor I knew the market value of the painting. One lesson I've learned as a collector is to never sell something before you are certain of its value. To establish value takes research. For some reason I didn't pay attention to this rule recently.

About forty years ago, I bought a painting at an auction for fifty dollars. It was an illustration art painting, signed with Joseph Christian Leyendecker's monogram. The subject was a Betsy-Ross-type revolutionary woman knitting, while her beau, dressed in military garb with a sword, was holding the yarn between his outstretched arms. At the woman's feet was a cute cat taking a nap. The year 1776 was painted above their heads. It was well painted and seemed to be authentic. Leyendecker paintings were not very popular when I bought it. I thought it could be authentic but I wasn't sure.

Over the years I had my doubts about its authenticity, so it remained buried in one of my art storage rooms. In the past twenty years or so, Norman Rockwell illustrations have sky-rocketed in price, especially his *Saturday Evening Post* covers. Major collectors include the movie directors George Lucas and Stephen Spielberg. Back about forty years ago, you could have bought a nice Rockwell for about $5,000. About ten years ago, a friend of mine was paying up to $400,000 for the Rockwells he began to collect. I thought he was crazy. Now the Rockwells are selling in the millions.

Rockwell's prices have shot to the moon, as high as $46,000,000 at a Sotheby's auction in 2013 for his painting "Saving Grace." As a result, Leyendecker paintings, most of them *Saturday Evening Post* covers, are quickly gaining in value because they are still available for reasonable prices compared to Rockwells.

Billi and I decided to put some art up for auction to gain more space and realize some extra cash.

We invited an auctioneer, who is a friend and one of the best and most honest auctioneers in New England, to our house. We picked out items, including a major Stephen Huneck secretary desk, which the auctioneer then advertised in a national art magazine. For some reason, which I cannot explain, I put the inadequately-researched Leyendecker in the auction. The auctioneer did some research and described it as "possibly Leyendecker" in his brochure. This meant he was not guaranteeing it.

Even though we knew he was an important artist, ridiculously, neither of us did the proper research to have an expert authenticate the painting. Late in the day, it finally came up at the auction. The 500th item in an auction is not exactly where you should place a valuable art work. The auctioneer started the bidding at $300. It quickly rose to the final winning bid of $6,750.

At first I was elated because the bidding was so high for a painting I bought in the 1970s for $50. Then I thought the buyer must know something I didn't know. On the ride home Billi and I were back to being elated about the sale and hoping the buyer wouldn't try to get his money back.

All during the next month we waited for the check from the auctioneer, which finally came and was deposited in the bank. This was a tidy profit for a fifty-dollar investment many years ago. A few weeks later I saw an ad in the New York Times for an auction at Heritage auctions in New York City. The ad showed a Leyendecker illustration painting with an estimated price of $100,000 to $150,000. It was a Thanksgiving Saturday Evening Post cover. This caught my attention and for some reason I decided to Google Leyendecker. Of course, I should have done this simple research before I put the painting to auction, but I didn't. After a few minutes, I found the Heritage painting that was in the ad and after scrolling down a bit more, I found the image of my painting. It was the Saturday Evening Post cover for July 4, 1931.

I immediately thought my painting was authentic and here was the proof. I bought the painting forty years ago and it seemed to have enough age on it to have been painted in 1931. It all made sense to me now. I should have Googled it before putting it into the auction, but I did not. Huge mistake. I further reasoned that no one would have copied the image because a Leyendecker was not very valuable before I bought it.

For a few weeks I could not get this colossal blunder out of my mind. I decided to call the auctioneer and tell him my finding. He said he had inquiries on the painting from a few so-called experts. An illustration auction house from New Jersey looked at it and declared it a copy. They said the canvas itself was made in the 1950s. They also said varnish was put on the painting to mask its age. Then again, they could have been putting up a smoke screen in order to buy it cheap at auction.

My auctioneer said he thought it may have been copied in the 1950s by an illustration art student. For these reasons my auctioneer listed the painting as "possibly by Leyendecker" to protect himself from liability as to its authenticity. He personally thought it was a copy. I felt a little bit relieved but I was still not totally convinced that it was a copy.

This got me to thinking. If I could buy it back for the $6,750 I received for it, would I do it and take the gamble again? Did I sell an authentic painting too cheap, or did I get a lot of money for a good copy? Because I no longer owned the painting, I could not show it to more experts for an opinion. If I could buy it back and it was proven absolutely to be a fake, I would forfeit the $6,750. What a dilemma.

I decided to talk to the buyer and maybe find out about the painting's authenticity. I asked the auctioneer to give the buyer my phone number. I could then talk to him about maybe buying the painting back. It turned out to be a moot point because the buyer never called me back. This made me think the painting was authentic. To this day I do not know if the painting is a copy, but my gut feeling is that the painting is authentic.

Some years ago I read an account of two newly-successful authors, who due to their recent success as writers were invited to a fabulously-rich businessman's estate.

When they arrived, the businessman had not yet appeared. A servant told them to walk the grounds of the magnificent estate and enjoy the famous sculptures of Botero and many other great artists until the owner arrived.

After a tour of the grounds and the garage loaded with the most expensive cars ever made, one of the authors exclaimed how wonderful it must be to live this magnificently with all this great stuff. The other author said, "I have something he doesn't have." The first author asked, "What is that?" The other author simply said, "I have enough."

Bobby and Billi in one of their art galleries, 2011
Credit: Jeb Wallace-Brodeur for *Seven Days*

Ronald Slayton, *Burlington Gothic (Pie in the Sky)*, 1937.
Oil on canvas, 27.5 x 19.5 in.

Ronald Slayton, *On the Way to Town (Weston)*, 1936.
Oil on Homasote, 19.75 x 15.75 in.

Philip Hagopian, *Picture on the Wall*, 1988.
Oil on canvas, 72 x 48 in.

Philip Hagopian, *Yo (Barnyard Homies)*, 2005.
Oil on canvas, 48 x 36 in.

Tom Deininger, *The Three Sisters*, 1998.
Found object assemblage, 96 x 96 x 8 in.

Tom Deininger, *Vermont Foliage: Out of the Landfill into the Woods*, 2007.
Found object assemblage, 96 x 96 x 32 in.

Francis Colburn, *Geranium*, 1955.
Oil on canvas, 32 x 22 in.

John Matusz, *The Kiss*, 1994.
Stone and steel, 92 x 60 x 29 in.

Tom Deininger, *Self Portrait*, 2006.
Found object assemblage, 96 x 60 in.

Tom Deininger, *Stroking Monet*, 2007.
Found object assemblage, 72 x 72 x 36 in.

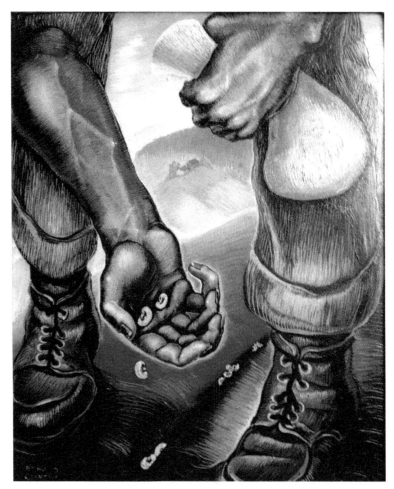

Ronald Slayton, *The Planter*, 1937.
Oil on canvas, 24 x 20 in.

Anton Doll, *Winter Skaters*, 1860.
Oil on canvas, 24.5 x 42.5 in.

Ronald Slayton, *The Last Supper*,
1985. Watercolor, 60 x 120 in.

Stephen Huneck, *CEO Sideboard*, 1990.
Carved basswood and oil paint, 90.5 x 69.5 x 20.5 in.

Bobby and Billi standing in front of Tom Deininger's *Plastic Paradise*, 2000.
Found object assemblage, 12 x 20 ft.

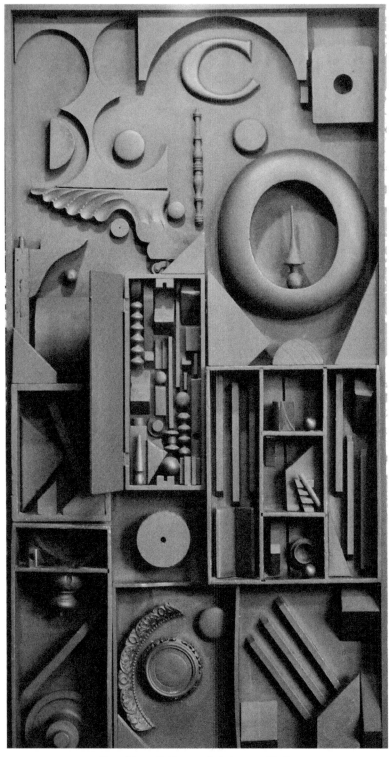

Jane Farrell, *Door to Infinity*, ca. 1977.
Found wooden object assemblage, 60 x 30 x 6 in.

Maurits Cornelis Escher, *House of Stairs*, 1951.
Lithograph 22/40, 47.2 x 23.8 cm.

Ronald Slayton, *Family Portrait*, 1991.
Oil on Homasote, 72 x 48 in.

23

BOOK STORIES

When we still had the antique store, there was an auction in a house across the street. I bought twenty boxes of books for a dollar a box. When I got the boxes back to the store, a woman came in and asked me if she could look through the boxes. I agreed and a short time later she came over to me with a leather-bound book. She asked if she could buy it. I told her nothing was for sale until I inventoried it and researched the value.

She told me she was related to the family whose belongings were being auctioned off. The book was a bound collection of all the handwritten letters a member of the family wrote to his mother from the battlefields of the Civil War. I could not understand why a woman would not invest twenty dollars at the auction to buy the books, if she knew this valuable family heirloom was in one of the boxes. I allowed her to take the book home for a few days to look at it. The book, which I still have today, is worth about $1,000.

Also in the boxes, I found a first edition by Charles Dickens and many other valuable books. I kept the most valuable books, which were worth about $2,500 and sold the remainder in the antique store. Eventually, I realized a profit of over $3,000 from a twenty-dollar investment. That venture greatly stirred my interest in old and rare books.

Books and art have become my joy and an investment. I can't hang a stock certificate on my wall and get any pleasure. I get pleasure from books and art. Besides, Wall Street is nothing but a big casino. This is a safer—and more beautiful—bet. I value old things like rare books because they are a legacy of the past. So little lasts forever in this infinite world of ours. But this is something solid I can hold in my hands and imagine all the people of past generations who also held it.

While exploring a rare bookshop in Newport, Rhode Island, in the late seventies, I noticed many newly- bound leather books. I asked the proprietor who bound the books. He told me the binder was Russell DeSimone, who lived in the area. The owner of the bookshop graciously gave me his phone number. I called him and our relationship began with Russell repairing some bindings for me. I found out later that bookbinding was his serious hobby. He was a classified systems analyst, working on nuclear submarine warfare for the United States Navy. Russell is an expert with a wide knowledge of rare books and broadsides. I have been fortunate to be the receiver of much book expertise from Russell.

I attended an auction at the home of a deceased amateur bookbinder. For $450 I bought a few garbage bags full of leather of all colors and sizes, about fifty hand-marbled English endpapers from the 1950s, some book clamps, and a filing cabinet that held the end papers. I took it all to Russell and asked his opinion on what it was worth. He said the value of the leather and the endpapers was over $10,000. From then on,

Russell has bound and repaired many books for me, using my own materials. Russell taught me a lot about books. He introduced me to fore-edge books. The edges of the pages are covered with gilt, but when you fan and hold the pages, a watercolor painting appears like magic. They are an extremely rare, one-of-a-kind example of exquisite bookmaking craftsmanship.

I was in a gift shop in Nantucket where I saw a two-volume set of William Cowper's poems from 1798. Inside the front cover, I saw a price of $240. From my experience, I valued the two volumes at about seventy-five dollars. Wondering why they would be so expensive, I noticed the gilt on the page edges. I fanned the pages of the first volume, and a gorgeous watercolor painting appeared. It depicted a block-long building in London, with soldiers marching, people walking, horses and carriages, and dogs in the street. I fanned the second volume and another similar scene magically appeared. I couldn't believe my find. My heart raced. Obviously, the shop owner didn't know what he had or the books would have been priced at a few thousand dollars because of the fore-edge paintings.

I had been in the shop before and overheard the owner bragging to another dealer about how he found a valuable object in a little old lady's yard sale and bought it cheaply and made a large profit. I figured the $240 price on the two volumes was from many years ago, priced by someone who had discovered the fore-edge paintings. I walked up to the woman tending the shop and said I would buy the books for the $240 price. She said the books were just for decor and not for sale. Now I knew for sure that the owner had no clue that the books were fore-edge or he would not have used these valuable volumes as display props.

I asked the clerk to tell the owner I would buy the books for $240. She said he would be back later and she would tell him. I returned later that day and she said I could have the books for that price. I couldn't hand her my credit card fast enough. If the shop owner were a little old lady, I would have told her the value of the books. But since the shop owner had bragged about taking advantage of the little old lady at her yard sale, I decided he had it coming. I was greatly rewarded for my knowledge of fore-edge books, which I learned from my friend Russell. From that moment on, I became a serious fore-edge book collector.

Every time I bought a fore-edge, Russell would make a custom box for it from my inventory of leather and endpapers. I was able to amass a collection of twenty-one fore-edge books before I surrendered my addiction to rising prices.

Throughout the years, I have scoured bookshops looking for treasures, developing a large library of rare books. In the 1980s my friend Peter Hill found a drug store in Schenectady, New York, with about seventy feet of beautiful oak bookcases for sale. I traded some architectural antiques I had with Peter, getting the bookcases in return. I hired a carpenter who spent 100 hours refitting them into my library. I finally had great shelf space to house my growing collection. I have collected many leather-bound sets of the works of the great authors and fine bindings on various authors and subjects, which are becoming harder to find year after year. Beautiful bindings are still possible to buy for a few hundred dollars apiece. To duplicate such a binding, if you could find someone skilled enough to do it, would cost a thousand dollars or more.

Some of my treasures include a first edition by Sir Walter Scott, with a letter handwritten by him in 1819–complete with his red wax seal, and a signed, first edition of Anais Nin's self-published *House Of Incest* about her affair with her father. I have a set of Don Quixote older than the set in George Washington's library and books from the 1500s. I can touch a book that was touched by people over 500 years ago. I have

An example of a fore-edge painting, which is painted on the edges of the pages of a book

Bobby in his rare book library and office, 2015
Credit: Josh Himes

a two-volume set of *Uncle Tom's Cabin* from the first year it was published and an unexpurgated, pirated edition of *Lady Chatterley's Lover* from the year it was published, 1928, in Florence, Italy. My greatest book hit was the recent auction acquisition of sixteen volumes of Napoleon in the finest full-leather, decorated bindings I have ever seen. Each volume contains an original letter pertaining to Napoleon, tipped in, including one signed by Napoleon. My research so far shows a market value of over $15,000. I paid $1,900. Not a bad investment.

I collect very little fiction except for Bibles. As an atheist, I have a collection of close to fifty rare Bibles. At least three dozen are the huge, heavy panel-covered family Bibles up to six inches thick. They were beautifully made in the 1800s, bound in full leather with gold-leaf engraved illustrations and titles on the covers. They are loaded with colored and black-and-white engravings inside. Some of them would cost thousands of dollars each to duplicate today if that were even possible. The irony is that I am an atheist—but I am also a booklover.

In this digital age, rare books and bindings are becoming even scarcer. They are fun to collect, read, and look at, besides being a great investment. What exists now is it. Throughout my life, rare-book collecting has given me much pleasure. Besides being an incredible source of reference and entertainment, books in a home library warm up the room and give it character. You can get a good idea of who a person is by observing the books in his or her library.

Sometimes I imagine a cartoon of a beautiful library with shelves completely bare, except for one thing: a single electronic book. Need I say anything more?

24

WHY I AM AN ATHEIST

The word God is for me nothing more than the expression and product of human weakness, the Bible a collection of honorable, but still primitive legends which are nevertheless pretty childish.
 —Albert Einstein, "The God Letter," 1954

I still believe that the major processes of the universe proceed according to the laws of physics; that they have no reference to our wishes, and are likely to involve the extinction of life on this planet; that there is no good reason for expecting life after death; and that good and evil are ideas which throw no light upon the nonhuman world.
 —Bertrand Russell, 1927

I do not believe in immortality of the individual, and I consider ethics to be an exclusively human concern with no superhuman authority behind it.
 —Albert Einstein, 1953

Scientific research is based on the idea that everything that takes place is determined by laws of nature, and therefore this holds for the actions of people. For this reason, a research scientist will hardly be inclined to believe that events could be influenced by a prayer, i.e. by a wish addressed to a supernatural being.
 —Albert Einstein, 1936

Religions are all alike—founded upon fables and mythologies.
 —Thomas Jefferson

Religious devotion capitalizes on the believer's fear and ignorance. Clerical pretention and corruption are vulgar deceptions allowed by custom, ignorance or personal gain.
 —Francisco Goya, *Los Caprichos*, 1799

The universe that we observe has precisely the properties we should expect if there is, at bottom, no design, no purpose, no evil, and no good, nothing but blind, pitiless indifference.
 —Richard Dawkins *River Out of Eden: A Darwinian View of Life*, 1995

I'm an atheist and I thank God for it.
 —George Bernard Shaw

I believe that all humanity, all the things humanity occupies its time with, and the Earth itself are as insignificant to the universe and its entire realm of inhabitants, as all the ants in an ant hill, all the things the ants occupy their time with, and the ant hill itself are as insignificant to the Earth and all humanity.

If the ants had intelligence and came up with the concept of an ant God, it would be a meaningless but comforting myth for the ants to pass around the hill. If you completely destroy the ants and the ant hill, all other life on Earth, and the Earth itself would still exist. When the hill is destroyed and all the ants are dead, the concept of the ant God no longer exists. Earth and humanity have no knowledge of what just happened and could care less.

The following thought exercise aids me in dismissing the God concept as the answer to the cosmic question. If something happened to instantly and totally destroy the Earth and all of humanity, like a collision with something from outer space or a human-triggered nuclear holocaust, all our galaxy and all the other galaxies in the universe would continue to exist with all their possible life-forms and their concepts for answering (or feeling or whatever they do) the cosmic question. The universe would continue undisturbed with its secret, with humanity out of the equation, and do quite well without a trace of the earth or utterance of the forgotten God concept. You have to imagine the universe without humanity to divorce yourself from religious thought and faith.

If the Earth and humanity never existed by chance, then religion and faith would never have been imagined, conceived, and developed, and the entire universe would still exist. If this were the case, where is your God?

A 2014 poll conducted by the Pew Research Center found that almost half of Americans would not approve of a family member marrying an atheist. The poll found that more than half of Americans would vote for a marijuana user, a lesbian, or an adulterer before voting for an atheist. So I know I'm not making a popular argument here. According to articles in their state constitutions, seven states still say you must believe in God to hold public office, even though the Supreme Court in 1961 ruled against having a "religious test" for public office. No state politician wants to be the first to shoot down these illegal state constitutional articles, which are not enforced.

Carl Sagan once said that Nietzsche and Einstein believed that what people call God is the sum total of all the physical laws of the universe. That is what I believe. Creationists believe that God created the universe by means of intelligent design. If what Nietzsche and Einstein believed is true, then the physical laws are the intelligence. The intelligence developed by means of the evolution of the universe. I believe that the continuing intelligence of evolution is the designer of the constantly expanding universe. Instead of accepting this fact backed by science, the creationists perpetuate the God myth and all the Bible stories to explain the cosmic question to nonthinkers and wrap it up in a faith-based, easy-to-understand package.

The package usually includes rules, costumes, music, ceremonies, architecture, the direction you should take with your personal and sex life, the feeling that you belong to something bigger than yourself if you obey all the rules, and much more. The belief of intelligent design and this package took hold of humanity thousands of years ago. Darwin published *On the Origin of Species* in 1859, which changed the general thinking of scientists by introducing the science-based theory of evolution.

Belief, faith, and myth had a huge advantage and organized hold on the belief systems of human beings long before the idea of evolution was born. A creationist can pray, pontificate, make up stories, and use faith as tools to disprove any proven scientific physical law of the universe. This can only end up fruitless in the eyes of a scientific thinker.

If creationists believe in intelligent design, I assume they don't use the same definition of the word intelligence, as I do. They use the word intelligent to equate faith with intelligence. Having intelligence means a person has the ability to think. If you really do think, how can you possibly accept the faith-based God answer to the cosmic question? Science uses intelligence, not faith, to attempt to answer the cosmic question. Therefore, I believe that creationists have shot themselves in the foot. If they believe in intelligent design, there is no room for faith in the equation. The only explanation I believe is the intelligence of evolution, and the expanding evolution of intelligence. I believe that evolution is the creator, creating by chance, not by design.

How can someone believe in intelligent design and not use their intelligence to examine the scientific evidence before they come to a faith-based conclusion to answer the cosmic question? I consider intelligent design an oxymoron. To a scientific thinker, belief in a religion and the Bible as proof that a creator intelligently designed the universe and everything in it (in six days according to Genesis) is insulting to human intelligence.

I think of it this way: Take the human out of the universe, and you take out the God.

While I believe at this time in the history of evolution, the human brain has not advanced enough to completely understand the scientific answer to the cosmic question, I further believe that the answer is definitely not religious belief.

Believers are students of the Bible. I am a student of the universe.

With this book I have come out of the marijuana closet, but there is one more closet I wish to leave, and that is the closet of atheism. I believe that the greatest gift Billi and I gave our children, Erik and Kristina, other than life itself, was not indoctrinating them into any religion. When Kristina was eight years old, she said she was "going to the library to see if the Bible was in the fiction or non-fiction section." She reasoned that if it was in the fiction section, then that would prove that "the Bible is a fib and not true." If only it were that simple.

When our son Erik was in the first grade in 1974, we got a call one day from the American Civil Liberties Union (ACLU), of which Billi and I were and still are members. They said Erik's teacher was having the students recite the Lord's Prayer every morning and the ACLU had received complaints from some parents. This was news to Billi and me as Erik never mentioned it. Because we were members, the Vermont ACLU asked us to meet with the teacher to request that she stop reciting the prayer as a first step to avoid legal action.

Billi and I met with the teacher, who was a very nice almost-retired lady. We told her that she was conducting a morning prayer against the Supreme Court decision on prayer in the schools. She told us, "I just can't stand the thought of my children [her students] not getting the word of the Lord." Nonetheless, she consented to stop the morning prayer. Billi and I and the ACLU were happy with the outcome.

I believe that prayer is wishful thinking. Late one night when Erik was in high school, I was awakened by a phone call from a parent whose young daughter had been to a play rehearsal with our son. He was distraught because his daughter left the rehearsal around 11:00 P.M. and was still not home. He wanted to know if my son knew where she was. I woke up Erik and he said he knew nothing of her whereabouts. When I got back on the phone, the wife answered and told me her husband just went out with the police to look for her daughter. I said I was sorry my son couldn't give any helpful information about her daughter and I didn't know what I could do to alleviate her problem. She said there was something I could do, and that was to pray for her daughter's safe return.

I figured that the daughter was somewhere in the back seat of her boyfriend's car. No matter where she was, there was no way that prayer would change it. The next day Erik told me she was with her boyfriend. I would guess the mother thought her prayers were answered because her daughter returned home safely. She was probably not too happy with what might have happened between her daughter and her boyfriend. The outcome could have been much worse. I believe that prayer would not have changed any of that.

Around 1999 Billi and I were visiting our daughter Kristina in Chicago. Her then boyfriend was driving his car and I was in the passenger seat. Kris was sitting in the back seat. Billi was not with us. The three of us were just stopping for a red light on Michigan Avenue when we heard a loud bump that shook the car. My first thought was that a small meteor struck the hood of the car and bounced off. I opened the door carefully and walked to the front of the car. What I saw was horrific. A man in shorts was lying in shock and trembling, spastically and violently near the left front of the car.

I knelt down beside him, trying to comfort him, and stupidly said, "You'll be alright." About thirty seconds later, two men in suits appeared and said, "You didn't hit him. He jumped off the eleventh floor of the Bloomingdale building."

The police came and said they would have to impound the car for a few hours and question Kris's boyfriend because he was the driver. The man was trying to commit suicide. The two guys in suits were Bloomingdale security guards and had tried to talk the guy out of jumping. He was copycatting a jumper who successfully killed himself the week before in the same spot.

If our car had been just a few feet ahead, the jumper would have landed on the roof. He would have indented the roof with his weight, possibly killing the driver and me. I called the hospital where the jumper was taken. They said he died a few hours after arrival.

I'm sure a religious believer would have thanked God if he was sitting in my seat and survived. I'm certain the believer would have thanked God for landing the jumper on the hood instead of the roof of the car. As an atheist I attribute our survival strictly to space, time, and universal chance, with no "thank-you-God prayer" necessary. We were simply one second and a few feet from the wrong place at the right time, in an unfortunate incident. It was just another chance happening in the universe. I think we were fortunate to miss possible death by one second.

I do not believe in life after death. I believe the brain is like a radio that receives and transmits information. When you smash the radio, it can no longer receive and transmit. When the body dies, whether it rots or is cremated, the brain can no longer receive and transmit information. I do not believe that when you die, a spirit or soul leaves the body and wanders into the universe or into another being. Einstein said, "Neither can I nor would I want to conceive of an individual that survives his physical death. Let feeble souls, from fear or absurd egoism, cherish such thoughts." Astrophysicists tell us we are made of "star stuff," (the remnants of exploding stars). I believe that the human ashes or remains eventually become mixed with earth to return to inanimate "star stuff." Life is temporary. When any living thing dies, it's all over, finished, kaput.

To comfort a child whose dog had just died, Pope Francis declared In December 2014, "One day, we will see our animals again in the eternity of Christ. Paradise is open to all of God's creatures." Because I believe that the concept of religion was invented to control people and make them feel good (you'll go to heaven) or bad (you'll go to hell), Francis, in his statement, just adds to the fact that religions make this stuff up as they go along.

Over the centuries, popes have wrestled with the question of animals going to heaven: Do animals have a soul or not? Popes continue to debate this animal question to this day, even though Pope Pious in 1854 declared the doctrine of papal infallibility, another joke.

My take on the Pope Francis statement: If paradise is open to all of God's creatures, then cats, all wild animals, all denizens of the deep in all the oceans and bodies of water, all insects (even mites and fruit flies)—in other words, all living creatures on earth—must go to heaven. Heaven must be one hell of a crowded place with all the quadrillions of creatures who have lived on Earth since the beginning of time now residing there.

Of course, some of them, the bad ones, must have gone to hell; especially mosquitoes and bad dogs. I hope lobsters go to heaven because they taste so good. Maybe some future pope will extend the entry into heaven to microbes, bacteria, and viruses. On second thought, they would have to go to hell because they could potentially wipe out the entire human race.

I don't believe in heaven or hell, but I believe the memories, mind, and spirit of the dead person live on in the minds of others, and in literature, music, art, and other creations, depending on the reputation of the deceased, and that is it. The deceased is either remembered as good (heaven) or bad (hell).

The following thought exercise aids me in imagining the infinite expanse of the universe: Imagine that this O is a scale model of the size of the Earth, and that this book represents an approximate scale model of the Milky Way Galaxy. Every single letter (except the O) and every molecule and atom on every page represent the more than 100 billion stars and objects in the Milky Way. Other than this book, all the buildings and their contents on the face of the Earth shall represent all of the remaining hundreds of billions of galaxies and stars in our known universe. All the buildings represent galaxies and all the objects in those buildings represent the stars in those galaxies. To take this visualization even further, all of the universe outside of our actual Earth shall represent the unknown universe beyond our observable universe. As complicated as it is, this total visualization helps me to imagine the incredible and infinite size of our known and unknown universe, even better than looking at all the pictures of parts of the universe we see in books and the media. (See accompanying "Thought Exercise" diagram at the end of this chapter). Even more mind-boggling, there are several theories that suggest that multiple universes exist beyond our universe.

Even with the inaccuracies of my extremely unscientific and very rough scale model visualization and thought exercise, we start to get a good idea of the infinite expanse of the universe in which we live, and the insignificance of the Earth itself. Our little O on the page is just a tiny speck. By picturing these vast distances in your mind, it would seem to be a reasonable assumption that there may be many other opportunities for life-forms in our galaxy and the rest of our known universe, without even mentioning the unknown universe, or the possible multi-universes.

I know this thought exercise is complicated and will be dismissed by many people, but it is easier for me to imagine the distances from one atom or molecule to every physical object on Earth than it is to imagine the distances between all the objects in the universe. It is intended to stir your mind while thinking about the possibilities of other life-forms in the universe. It works for me and I hope it helps you.

As human beings, we wonder where we came from, how we were created, and what the purpose of our existence is. In order to explain our creation, existence, and purpose on earth, the most popular concept we have come up with is the concept of God. Some version of God created the Earth and the universe and ourselves. I refer to this as the God concept that was conceived by the human brain. Genesis states that our universe was created by God in six days. Our present concept of the universe did not exist when the Bible was written.

If you are a believer (creationist) or an agnostic (I don't know), I suggest you read or reread Genesis. Then, skim through any of the great books on the universe as we know it today, preferably with telescopic pictures of the cosmos. Now try to put your mind in neutral, clear of any religious doctrine, and rethink your belief system.

How can you read the first few chapters and verses of Genesis without maybe thinking they would fit well into Grimm's fairytales, after having at least a miniscule knowledge of and exposure to science, physics, and astronomy?

Scientific thinking will advance when it disproves an old theory with newly discovered information about the cosmos. Religions will continue the same old dogma, belief system, and thinking throughout the ages and in perpetuity. Believers prefer to obey authority rather than think for themselves and make up their own minds about the answer to the cosmic question. Believers are conditioned and brainwashed to accept the certainty of their religion, which is based on faith, myths, and stories only. Doubt is not tolerated. Physical laws of the universe are provable, when discovered. Faith is unprovable. Believers mistake coincidence as a positive answer to a prayer. When a prayer is not answered, it is God's will.

Everything man has made on Earth is a result of science and the evolution of the mind, not by the mindless following of faith. It is all made possible because of the discovery of some of the physical laws of the universe and understanding and applying them. If you depended on faith alone, while ignoring science, nothing much would be made and we would still be living in the Stone Age. Christian Scientists (another oxymoron) ignore proven medical treatment, preferring to use faith and prayer to heal the sick. The result: Many of them die.

Philip Appleman in his essay, "God, Darwin, and the Meaning of Life" in *The Scientific Examination of Religion: The Best of Free Inquiry* (published by the Council for Secular Humanism) said, "People in general have never exhibited much passion for the disciplined pursuit of knowledge, but they are always tempted by easy answers. God is an easy answer. God is a term that deliberately masks our ignorance. Learning is hard work, imagining is easy. Given our notorious capacity for indolence, is it any wonder that school is so unpopular, faith so attractive?"

Now let us imagine the myriad possibilities for other human and nonhuman life-forms and their concepts alien to ours, which could possibly exist in places and dimensions in all the other billions of galaxies, each made up of billions of stars. If any of them had intelligence, they could come up with their own reasons for their existence and their own answers as to how the universe was created. Maybe they could sense their reasons in ways far beyond our human imagination and comprehension. Could there even be plants and animate forms that "know and feel" way more of the universe than we could ever know? If the chemicals in many plants expand our minds, what do they do for the plant itself?

The chance that we are alone in our galaxy and the universe seems to me to be very remote. Other objects in our universe and beyond that do not mirror our Earth with the elements that support life here could harbor other unimaginable life-forms and intelligence. Somewhere in the over 100 billion stars in our galaxy alone, it would seem possible to support other intelligent life-forms.

In light of these seemingly infinite possibilities for extraterrestrial life, it seems presumptuous for humanity to think that it has the answer to the cosmic question all figured out with the God concept. For me, the word God is a loaded word. When it is used to discuss all the physical laws of the universe, it is polluted and not useful at all. The vision of a wise, old divine guy with a beard, sitting on a throne up in heaven does not cut it for me. There is no up or down in the universe, so where is this God? Of course, there has to be some unknown universal force existing to answer the cosmic question. Could it be a huge blob of protoplasm at the center of everything, rather than a supreme being? I think that the human mind will never find the answer to the cosmic question if it continues to believe in myths and fables.

This brings me to a major point I would like to make. Some people persist in seeking enlightenment through words of fallible origin, handed down from human to human. I believe that to know and be enlightened about the ultimate truth of the universe, it could be experienced or known by a feeling that is impossible to be described and taught with words. Knowledge might be gained by tuning into a frequency with your mind that connects you to a universal knowledge, in a way similar to how information is passed wirelessly on the internet.

Your brain is an organic computer. Could tinnitus (ringing in the ears), with or without drugs, be the brain receiving an audible universal frequency wave, allowing the brain to connect with and interpret universal knowledge? Why would this thought be more ridiculous than having faith in any religion or spirituality to explain the unknown? From my experience, ringing in the ears often exists at the height of euphoria after ingesting marijuana and other drugs. Could it be a universal frequency? If the universal frequency did in fact exist, how would the brain learn to plug into it? Or is it just a noise generated inside of an individual's brain? At the very least, the ringing in the ears is a provable fact. The question is this: Could it be a connection to universal knowledge? My in-and-out-of-body hallucinatory experiences under the influence of peyote, LSD, and marijuana were often accompanied by ringing in the ears.

Marijuana and other hallucinogenic drugs could be a gateway to expanding the mind and preparing it to receive such a frequency, if in fact it does exist. This thinking is a longshot, which many people will laugh at, but it makes more sense to me than the God concept. If you ever experienced hallucinogenic drugs, and traveled in your mind to outer space, while hearing frequencies in your mind, you might give this concept some serious thought. I believe that the answer to the cosmic question is truly beyond words.

My frequency-based thoughts on transmitting universal knowledge do not seem so far out when you consider the brilliant inventor and futurist Raymond Kurzweil's singularity theory. The *singularity* is the time when artificial intelligence surpasses the human intellect. According to Wikipedia, "Kurzweil describes his law of accelerating returns, which predicts an exponential increase in technologies like computers, genetics, nanotechnology, robotics, and artificial intelligence."

He says this will lead to a technological singularity in the year 2045, a point where progress is so rapid it outstrips humans' ability to comprehend it. Kurzweil predicts the technological advances will irreversibly transform people as they augment their minds and bodies with genetic alterations, nanotechnology, and artificial intelli-gence. Once the singularity has been reached, Kurzweil says that machine intelli-gence will be infinitely more powerful than all human intelligence combined. After-wards he predicts intelligence will radiate outward from the planet until it saturates the universe.

I must ask: Would the method of transmittal be frequency waves?

Stephen Hawking has said, "The development of full artificial intelligence could spell the end of the human race." Elon Musk said at MIT, "I think we should be very careful about artificial intelligence. If I had to guess at what our biggest existential threat is, it's probably that artificial intelligence would summon the demon." This is the stuff of science fiction. Could machines reproduce themselves and destroy hu-manity? Is this the evolutionary fate of life on Earth? Not a comforting thought, but one that we, our children, and their children's children will not have to deal with. In December 2015, Musk announced that he and a few other investors would establish a nonprofit, billion-dollar artificial intelligence research center named OpenAI to de-velop "digital intelligence" that will benefit humanity.

All of this seems to me to be far beyond the human concept of God. Considering the billions of objects in the universe, I believe it would be a mistake to think that earth is the only place with intelligence.

In a *Wall Street Journal* interview with Alexandra Wolfe on May 31, 2014, Kurz-weil said, "Human intelligence will be enhanced a billion-fold thanks to high tech brain-extensions." He further imagines, "Once our neocortices are connected to the cloud—something he expects to happen in the 2030s—this wireless connection will make us much smarter." On the downside, with our brains connected to the cloud, could other people or machines access the thoughts in your brain like hackers on the internet?

Kurzweil also said, "In some ways, we've already expanded our brains. When it comes to mobile devices like smartphones, for instance, philosophically I don't see a significant difference whether technology is inside your brain or whether my brain is directing my fingers. It's really an extension of my brain already, but we will make it more convenient by directly connecting it into our brains."

You must note that if all this happens, our brains will receive instant knowledge wirelessly on a frequency wave. So, to me, it is not much of a stretch to imagine that all universal knowledge (the answer to the cosmic question) could be transmitted on a frequency wave or waves from outer space and somehow get plugged into a cloud which would feed all intelligence wirelessly to our brain. Who knows, this could be already happening somewhere in the universe on a planet whose inhabitants have super intelligence.

If this sounds far-fetched to you, the technology already exists, when further de-veloped, to plug our minds into the cloud of all human intelligence.

In another interview with *Wall Street Journal* editor-in-chief Gerard Baker, Kurz-weil said, "A Parkinson's patient can actually download new software to the comput-er connected into their brain from outside the patient. It's pea-sized, so it requires minimally invasive surgery."

Now, imagine what intelligence may already be out there in some of the trillions of objects in the universe and beyond. As Richard Dawkins says, "It is easy to believe that the universe houses creatures so far superior to us as to seem like gods."

Imagine (like a science fiction writer) what is already out there and what will be out there in the future, as the universe evolves. I believe the possibility that universal knowledge is already floating out there on frequency waves and we have to figure out how to plug our brains into it.

It's all evolution, and the human brain could be joining with the computer in a singularity soon. Evolution is the Grand Supreme Designer.

Gopi Krishna described enlightenment as "Bathed in light and in a stage of exaltation and happiness impossible to describe." This sounds very much like some kind of hallucination to me. In other words, if he is correct, the answer to the cosmic question is beyond words. Since the human mind has evolved to its present complexity, can it also evolve further toward total enlightenment and cosmic understanding? Could hallucinogens aid us in this quest? Could plugging the mind into frequencies in the universe be a path to universal knowledge?

If, as Einstein believed, God in all its descriptions in the Bible is a product of childish legends, it would be mind-blowing to then realize how much time all of humanity has wasted killing people with religious wars and entertaining itself with these myths and legends throughout the centuries. I believe that all religions will eventually become obsolete as the human mind progresses and people abandon mythology to pursue intelligent thought.

According to the May 2015 Pew Center report on religion, Christians are losing about 1 percent of followers each year, dropping by almost 8 percentage points in seven years. Religiously unaffiliated people (also known as nones) have increased more than 6 percentage points in the last seven years. Christianity is losing about 1 percent a year while the unaffiliated are gaining almost 1 percent a year.

If this trend continues, Christianity could be obsolete in the next fifty to 100 years, especially if Kurzweil's super-human intelligence predictions come true.

Amazing Randi, the magician, supernatural debunker, well-known skeptic, and atheist was interviewed by Adam Higginbotham in an article in the *New York Times* on November 9, 2014. When asked why he believed other people needed religion, he responded, "They need it because they're weak, and they fall for authority. They choose to believe it because it is easy." He further said, "Science, after all, is simply a logical, rational, and careful examination of the facts that nature presents to us. I think that religion is a very damaging philosophy because it's such a retreat from reality."

Richard Dawkins, the well-known English atheist, wrote the following note to potential subscribers of *Free Inquiry*, the excellent skeptic's magazine published by the Council for Secular Humanism:

"Just for a moment, imagine that there really is a supreme being who created all things, including the human race. Would he (or she or it) give you such a highly developed brain and then punish you for using it?

Would the most advanced life-form in the universe devise such grand concepts as DNA, nuclear fusion, and quantum mechanics and then spend all eternity fussing about whether you regularly sing to him, vote against gay marriage, or accept on faith that Earth is only 6,000 years old when there is a mountain of evidence to the contrary?

Frankly, I don't believe in an all-knowing, all-powerful creator. But even if I did, I'm certain he would want us to think for ourselves and eschew such claptrap.

He would be committed to the application of reason and encourage scientific discovery and the cultivation of moral excellence. He would want us to be more concerned about living a valuable life than enforcing arbitrary rules to avoid a vindictive punishment in an afterlife."

I agree with Dawkins completely. I feel it only fair, however, to allow some time here for the agnostic viewpoint. The following is an exchange of letters between me and my cherished friend Marc A. vanderHeyden, Ph.D., a former member of a religious society and president emeritus of Saint Michael's College:

September 8, 2015

Dear Bobby,

First, I must thank you for the privilege of reading the manuscript of your memoir. It was a very interesting read with a few surprises and an equal number of confirmations of what your family and friends know of Bobby. Most of all, I ended with a genuine admiration of your candor in sharing your experience of a full—and clearly fulfilling—life. This was not a mere sharing of anecdotes but of your deep appreciation of family, music, arts, drugs, and above all your knowledge of the *self*. The latter may be the intent but is not always the outcome of memoirs. Here, however, we have a very open and frank "report card." Perhaps this is our impression because of your descriptions of drugs and drug use throughout and your singular chapter on atheism. It is the latter that compelled me to write since I want to react to your claim to be a "student of the universe."

It is no surprise to me that you began having troubles with religion at an early stage in life. Many young people have reacted adversely to their elders' call for forced participation in religious exercises and have maintained that dislike for a lifetime. To you, I surmise, it was also the foundation of what would grow into firm atheism.

When you describe your experiences with drugs—good and bad—you use language that reminds me of what some medieval mystics would write: the out-of-body experience, the voices from somewhere else, the call to the other side, communication with another power in the universe, etc. The use of peyote, marijuana, and many other drugs are often found in the history of religions and there, too, one can read that these hallucinogenic experiences expanded the mind and brought new insights or greater wisdom. These experiences were used to address the questions for which there were no scientific answers. They were tools to reach that wisdom, that great idea, that power in the universe, that divine power.

When you wrote that you also have found creative power and expansion of the mind in careful drug use, you point out that you did not reach the answers of ancient religions but, instead, they forced you to look earnestly to science. Therein, of course, we all find ourselves, as twenty-first-century people engrossed in the review and acceptance of evolution. You appear to make your juxtapositions to science/evolution primarily with "the Bible" people. That is for me too narrow. There are many religions within human history that are totally unaware and unrelated to the biblical stories. Whether we think of Hinduism, Zoroastrianism, Buddhism, animism, or Aztec religion, the reality is that only our Western world has had this exposure to the Bible and that there were varying degrees of acceptance and rejection of it throughout the ages.

I think that, fortunately, a growing number of people—and I admit I am thinking of the people who comprise our families and friends—are accepting of Darwin's theory of evolution, including the evolution of the human mind. Regretfully, we have too many in our own American society who refuse to welcome the insights and proofs of science and cling to biblical answers for cosmic questions.

Next time when we get together I want to hear some clarification of your "thought exercise," which leaves me somewhat dissatisfied. It leads rather too quickly to the ultimate question, which is "why is there anything at all?" This question has been my preoccupation for many years and that is one of several reasons why I took the opportunity to respond to your writing. Jim Holt wrote an interesting book on that very subject a few years ago where, indeed, he posits, "you might expect that science will someday explain not only how the world is, but why it is." To me it was somewhat disconcerting that he quotes an eminent scientist, Stephen Hawking, who asked, "Why does the universe go through all the bother of existing?"

When I was a student in Louvain in the early sixties, we heard quite a bit about the French Jesuit Teilhard de Chardin and his cosmology that included the evolution of the human in concert with the evolution of the universe. Our capacity to think is crucial in our search of comprehending the cosmos. We learned also about another Catholic priest, George Lemaitre who was a professor at the University of Louvain in the thirties and who had successfully proven Einstein's proposition of an expanding universe that led to what we now know as the Big Bang theory.

Atheists have never really liked or accepted the fact that the universe could have a beginning. It makes the "why question" even harder. Since science (so far) has not found good answers for what could have been before the Big Bang—if anything—many nonscientists have entered the debate.

I do not believe that we owe survival to chance; there must be some scientific principles that guide the evolution of and expansion of the universe and its contents.

You cite quite a few examples where religion really obfuscates matters, ignores science, creates evil, and brings nefarious consequences to an ignorant public. Religion is certainly a human creation and clearly designed to answer questions of all kinds: problems in nature or in organizations of society. Some religions may have been inspired by hallucinations, others by reflection, hope, or fear. I believe religion was created by the time our human ancestors became conscious of their existence. This to me remains the most impressive experience we have: That we are aware of our own mind! (I realize that I am clearly Cartesian but I cannot help but admire Descartes for his contributions even though he has lost his pivotal place in philosophy.)

In the early phases of our evolution there were thousands of questions that neither experience nor thought could fathom. The need for answers, the need for knowledge led to exploration as well as invention of solutions. These inventions included religion, which in turn became a paradigm for organization of societies and behaviors. Hundreds of gods and spirits, good and bad, were constructed to overcome ignorance. In this evolution we wait until the nineteenth and twentieth centuries to see the real atheism come to the fore as a result of scientific breakthroughs and answers, not in the least Darwin's contribution of evolution.

In a recent article in "Commonweal," (May 1, 2015) Gary Gutting wrote a review of Michael Ruse's book *Atheism—What Everyone Needs to Know*, in which he points to the "new atheists" like Dawkins, Harris, and Hitchens as the more aggressive attackers of religion and the voice of uncompromising atheism.

I like Gutting's warning: "How can anyone be that certain God does not exist?" That kind of firmness is more reminiscent of the dogmatism of the fundamentalist than the systemic pursuit of the scientist. I think that most of my religious friends would be prepared to admit that they do not *know* that God exists. That is why I like agnosticism even when Dawkins and others call that "wishy-washy." Agnosticism to me means a very reluctant acceptance of not knowing, of admitting to doubt, of keeping the mind open to advances in sciences and philosophy. I find it a very human stance that takes courage and humility.

You raise the possibility, actually the likelihood, that the road of enlightenment may proceed in another accelerated pace as a result of artificial intelligence and the potential of "technological singularity." There is, at this time, as much excitement as there are forebodings about this future. I believe the human mind will take this challenge in stride. I do not share your mixture of enthusiasm and pessimism on that score. I have always been more a student of humanity that a student of the universe. Perhaps I was insufficiently educated in the sciences or I lacked the confidence to tackle the vast subject of cosmology. Humanity, and particularly the history of humanity, has been my pleasure to pursue. I love the renaissance humanists who cherished the central place of mankind in this immense expanding universe. I am not unhappy about these shortcomings because it encourages me in a constant search for learning and the pursuit of wonder. I know you cherish that as much as I do. It makes a human human.

Thank you again for the privilege,

Marc

December 24, 2015

Dear Marc,

Thank you for your beautiful letter. I am flattered that you have considered my beliefs worthy of your comments, which are highly valued by me. They are exactly the scholarly tone I expected and certainly no surprise. You said you are more a student of humanity than a student of the universe.

I do love humanity, being alive, and have the greatest respect for all living things. I do stand firmly, however, by my atheism. But, here's the rub: In my day-to-day life, I am 100 percent tuned into humanity. In my independent thinking life, I leave humanity behind and am 100 percent tuned into the universe. I believe the two viewpoints have nothing to do with one another. Humans, a result of chance, can think and make choices. I believe the universe happens and evolves strictly by chance, not by design.

The immense universe expands outward from the Big Bang in a constant and wondrous evolution of explosions and beauty (humanity being one example). The universe, constantly changing, prevails, but humanity may not. We are simply the ants in an ant hill. You said you "do not believe that we owe our survival to chance; there must be some scientific principles that guide the evolution of and expansion of the universe and its contents."

For me that means design. I believe that humanity's survival depends on chance (the same as the life of each individual), not design. I do not believe there is a Grand Designer. No one will win the cosmic question argument. While you are on your "constant search for learning and the pursuit of wonder," I will join you.

I must say goodbye for now. I need to put the spider that just crawled across the floor, safely outside, where it can continue its journey in its universe, whatever that is.

With my deepest respect,

Bobby

Many years ago, I watched the late David Bowie, the singer, being interviewed on television. The interviewer asked, "I understand you are an atheist, so why are you wearing that large cross on a chain around your neck?" David answered, "Just in case."

THOUGHT EXERCISE: *WHY I AM AN ATHEIST*

This rough scale model helps me to imagine the infinite possibilities of other life forms in our known universe—and the unknown beyond.

This letter *O* represents Earth.

This book you are reading represents the Milky Way Galaxy.

Each building and structure on our planet represents an observable galaxy other than the Milk Way Galaxy.

All the objects inside these buildings and structures represent the planets and stars in these other observable galaxies.

In this way, the actual Earth represents all observable galaxies in our observable universe.

Our known universe represents everything beyond what we can observe: the unknown and possible multi-universes.

25

WHAT I HAVE LEARNED TO BELIEVE

Cannabis brings us an awareness that we spend a lifetime being trained to over-look and forget and put out of our minds.
—Carl Sagan

After over sixty years of on-and-off again use of marijuana, I have learned to believe the following: On first trying marijuana, one of four things usually happens. Some people don't get high because they didn't consume enough of it or didn't realize they were moderately high. Some people get high in some degree and enjoy the feeling. Some people have a bad experience from consuming too much the first time, which can result in paranoia or hallucinations, and scare off the experimenter. And some people experience various combinations of the first three responses.

As I said earlier in this book, the problems result mostly from lack of standardization of the potency of what they are consuming. First-timers must learn how to get high safely. It is sort of like learning to ride a bicycle. You can't just jump on and have a safe, nice ride. You must practice and gain experience. With marijuana, you must err on the side of conservatism and caution until you safely know what you are doing.

If you smoke the marijuana as a first-timer, rather than ingesting it, there is less chance to get in trouble. When you smoke the marijuana, you can go gradually, a puff or two at a time. You can start to feel the effect in a matter of minutes. You can control the effect by simply inhaling no more, if you like the way you feel. Beware that today's marijuana is extremely potent, and one puff could be enough to get even the most experienced user high. This is not your grandmother's pot. Today's marijuana can be ten to twenty times more potent than the weed they did at Woodstock in the 1960s. Unfortunately, smoking anything is extremely harmful to your health.

There is one method of smoking marijuana that I strongly suggest you avoid. That method is inhaling the vapors of "Butane Hash Oil" or BHO, which has become popular recently, especially with more experienced smokers. The media has called it "marijuana's explosive secret" and "the crack of marijuana." The process of manufacturing it makes the THC concentration as high as 90 percent. I would say most people experience an average THC potency of about 12 percent. Smoking concentrate is about as close as marijuana gets to smoking crack.

The marijuana is made into a concentrate by a process called "blasting." It is five to ten times more potent than regular marijuana. The process uses nasty solvents like N-butane, ethanol, benzene, and many others. It is extremely dangerous to make, similar to the hazards of a meth lab. The extract goes by various names, including "shatter," "honeycomb," "wax," and "budder."

The extract is smoked in a bong equipped with a "nail" adapter. With a "dabbing tool," you place a "dab" of extract ("shatter") on the "nail," which you heat up to 600 degrees with a small blowtorch. This produces a vapor that you inhale. This method of smoking marijuana is called "dabbing." You have to be nuts to participate in this conduct. This is for the user who wants to get extremely stoned. I don't think this is fun unless you really want to drop out of productive daily life and maybe become addicted. You might as well shoot heroin or become a crack head, in my opinion. Just when marijuana is gaining some respect, here comes "dabbing" with the potential to mess it all up.

I recently experimented with medical marijuana tinctures and found it to be a nice way to ingest the drug. You can easily control how much you use, a drop at a time, with an eye dropper. You can start with a few drops in your coffee, tea, or juice and increase the dosage as you become familiar with your tolerance, as you experiment. If glycerin or vegetable oils are used to make the extract, it should be safe to ingest.

If you want a quick course in understanding where the business of marijuana is today, pick up a copy of *High Times*, the marijuana magazine that's been around for forty years. I promise that it will blow your mind.

If you choose to do marijuana, I believe that the safest, healthiest, and most socially-friendly method to consume it is to ingest it. When you ingest the marijuana, however, you must still be very cautious. Once you have ingested an amount of pot, there is no turning back. It is in your system and cannot be reversed until it wears off. If you ingest too much, as I did when I was hospitalized in Newport, you can have serious consequences. I would not suggest ingesting marijuana to a first-time experimenter.

As much as I am against smoking it, as a first-timer, you could get in less trouble by taking a puff or two at a time until you know you are high, without going any further. Once you understand how you want to feel, next time you can experiment with conservatively ingesting a controlled amount of marijuana, knowing its potency. When you learn how much you want to ingest, abandon smoking it forever.

Even experienced marijuana users can get in trouble if, for some reason, they ingested an amount that was far more potent than they realized. The potency of a portion must be clearly marked and kept totally away from children. It should be illegal for medical marijuana clinics and legal stores to sell edibles that in any way resemble children's candy, like gummy bears and lollipops.

If in doubt about the potency of what you are going to ingest, always cut the recommended portion at least in half, before you consume it. I believe that your brain somehow files the amount of marijuana you consumed and builds a tolerance for it. I believe this tolerance varies with different people and changes according to the amount of usage over periods of time. I further believe that this is why two people may each react differently to consuming the exact same amount of the same pot.

Once you are in control of the potency of how much you consumed, you should then have a safe and pleasant high. I don't consider high a negative word. It is merely the safer euphoria a conservative recreational marijuana user seeks—in contrast to the various degrees of drunkenness a user of alcohol seeks.

I have noticed a timeline from my many years of experience ingesting cannabis. After ingesting a controlled amount, it takes about a half hour to one hour before I start to feel results, depending on when my mind plugs into what is happening to it. After about one hour, continuing up to about four hours, I feel a general euphoria before it gradually starts to recede over the next four to six hours. The whole experience can last about eight hours. During this time, I experience varying degrees of relaxation, euphoria, insightful and creative thoughts, and a general feeling of better understanding and perception of anything my mind decides to process. It also diminishes any pain I felt before consuming it. I believe it masks the pain to the point of not caring about it, rather than eliminating it. Marijuana helps me deal with and temporarily forget about my pain from arthritis.

Dr. Lester Grinspoon, an early authority on marijuana, said in an interview with Rick Cusick in *High Times* magazine in November 2014, "For many conditions, the analgesic effect of cannabis doesn't make the pain go away, but it puts it into the background." I sometimes think of it as having an itch, but feeling no need to scratch it. Under the influence of marijuana, I forget the pain (itch) is there. It seems to disappear from my mind. I am no longer conscious of it. I simply don't care about it.

At 5:00 P.M., when many people have a drink or two to wind down from their day, I may consume a cannabis cookie, which will ensure a pleasant, pain-free, insightful, creative, and euphoric evening of thought until bedtime around 11:30 P.M. It also allows me to review and analyze this totally screwed-up and crazy world as the theater of the absurd that it actually is, caused by all the various beliefs and actions of the human condition. Since Billi does not use marijuana, she may have a glass of wine.

I see marijuana at the center of the available drug spectrum. By this I mean the benefits greatly outweigh the downside. It is a safer and more intelligent high than nicotine or alcohol. It is more moderate than an opioid high, but without the possible consequences of addiction or death.

In my opinion, marijuana is the perfect drug for recreational use and treatment of all but the most severe forms of pain. It is the "ultimate twofer." Eating marijuana is the safe way, and I believe, the only way, to go for the person who desires a recreational high. Crossing the line into opioids becomes risky conduct. Marijuana is all I need.

The two main species are sativa and indica. Generally, sativas smell like flowers, and indicas smell like a skunk. The active psychoactive ingredient is tetrahydrocannabinol (THC). Besides pure sativa and pure indica, there are hundreds of strains and hybrids (cross breeds) of the two, and more are being developed daily by growers.

The sativas are more cerebral and energizing, and the psychoactive THC causes a more creative high. Indicas are more calming and relaxing and medically useful. One of the at least eight-five cannabinoid compounds in the marijuana plant is cannabidiol (CBD). A plant can be bred to contain CBD but very little or no THC. This is the strain that has helped some child epileptics reduce their seizures, without the psychoactive effects of THC.

If a person consumes alcohol most of his or her waking hours, that person is almost certain to become an alcoholic. If a person smokes or ingests marijuana most of his or her waking hours, that person is almost certain to become what I call a *marijuanic* and possibly mildly addicted. If the user is of the addictive type, stopping either may lead to some form of depression, at least temporarily. An alcoholic could experience delirium tremors (DTs). I do not believe that a "marijuanic" will experience anything so serious. Marijuana withdrawal is similar to stopping the drinking of coffee, at the worst. On the occasions when I stopped consuming marijuana for any period of time, I never had a negative experience. I never even had a headache, which I experienced sometimes when I stopped drinking coffee.

During the euphoric period, after ingesting too much cannabis, you now risk having hallucinations, paranoia, and a possible overdose, similar to my Newport hospitalization experience. There is a point at the highest peak of euphoria when your mind can become confused, when you are having certain thoughts. For a few seconds or minutes your mind could temporarily draw a complete blank as to what you were thinking. I believe that this is the point where a "marijuanic" could possibly cause changes in "working memory" brain structure. This may be especially true if the user's brain is still developing in the teenage years, and could be critical to memory and reasoning, according to researchers at Northwestern University's Feinberg School of Medicine, as reported by Mitchell S. Rosenthal in the *New York Times* on January 10, 2014.

According to Mark Miller in an article in the June 2015 *High Times* magazine, "A study conducted by the Harvard Medical School in 2005 used magnetic-resonance imaging on twenty-two habitual pot smokers and found no significant structural changes within their brains compared to non-users. Also, a 2011 Australian study found no link between long-term use and dysfunction.

The *New York Times* in an editorial on April 23, 2015, reported, "Nicotine can harm the developing adolescent brain and cause lasting cognitive damage." Alcohol can also cause brain damage.

If you experience a short-term memory blank while under the influence of marijuana and you concentrate, you should quickly regain your previous thoughts. However, this is the point where you could temporarily lose control of your mind, if you ingested too much marijuana or you smoke more. I believe this is the point where hallucination and paranoia begins along with a possible change in heart rhythms and other problems.

To eliminate this possibility, you must always know the potency of what you are consuming, and if you are already euphoric, do not consume more. Medical marijuana lists the percentage of THC it contains. This serves as a reference point for the user to figure out, from past experience, how much to safely consume. Legalized pot will list the same standards of THC potency, further ensuring the safety of the user. This is a great leap forward toward eliminating bad experiences with the drug for the general public. However, black market marijuana will still have a question remaining about its potency, as will home grown, unless the grower is familiar with the seeds or has a way of measuring the potency of the THC. The marketing of a THC test kit to the general public would be a helpful safety tool. The bottom line is always treat marijuana that you are unfamiliar with very cautiously.

You must learn where your line is between feeling euphoric enough and losing control, thus experiencing paranoia and hallucination. You must safely find the correct level of high that is safe and enjoyable for you with no downside. Everyone's perfect level is different as to how they respond to an amount of THC.

It must be noted that the abuse of prescription opioid drugs is a far more serious problem than marijuana abuse. As stated in the first chapter, at the top of the list of abused prescription opioids are OxyContin, oxycodone, hydrocodone, fentanyl, and many others, with death rates higher than heroin. Fentanyl is fifty times more powerful than heroin. It is often mixed with heroin on the street, resulting in many overdoses and deaths. Some people seem to have a genetic predisposition to addiction. Fortunately, I am not one of those people.

Drugs made from the poppy plant are called opiates and its synthetic versions are called opioids. The two terms are commonly used interchangeably according to what some doctors and pharmacists told me. According to *Consumer Reports*, 17,000 Americans a year die because of opioids. But, I have read other accounts of the numbers of opioid deaths per year being anywhere between 23,000 and 45,000. Whatever the real number is, it is a terrible death toll.

I believe that if you have ever hallucinated, you have experienced a small window into the unknown reaches of the mind. I am very grateful that I safely experienced hallucinating, after ingesting peyote and marijuana. As I said in the last chapter, I believe hallucination could hold a key to plugging your mind into the reality of the universe, but it can be a very scary place. With peyote my mind traveled far out into the universe where a God-like voice asked me to "cross over to the other side," which was frightening and which I took to mean death. This is the only time I ever got close to questioning my atheism and my belief that there is no afterlife after death. There must have been a particle of religious indoctrination left somewhere in my mind that my Grandmother Zeller instilled in me in my youth.

If what I was experiencing was, or could be, a reality of some sort, was the voice insinuating that if I accepted the voice's request to "cross over" (to death), there was something else "on the other side?" Even though I was obviously hallucinating, the whole episode seemed frighteningly real.

I felt that I was experiencing and understanding all the knowledge of the universe, but I still wished to remain where I had been living. When I recovered from the episode, I could no longer feel what I experienced and what seemed to be so real during the hallucination. I totally lost touch with my everyday physical reality and temporarily lost control of my mind. I was conscious of the line I had crossed over. It was extremely frightening and though I am grateful for the experience, I don't think I wish to go into that unknown place in my mind ever again. It was like my mind was traveling through the universe, but my physical body was still on Earth. I must ask: Could mind-altering drugs aid in the evolution of the brain's better understanding of the cosmic question?

Bruce Weber, in his June 8, 2014, *New York Times* obituary of psychedelic researcher Alexander Shulgin said that Shulgin had an epiphany "that it was possible to chemically extend the horizons of perception." Shulgin said, "I understood that our entire universe is contained in the mind and the spirit. We may choose not to find access to it, we may even deny its existence, but it is indeed there inside us, and there are chemicals that can analyze its availability."

Since I am an atheist, I wonder: Was the God-like voice I heard what believers would call God talking to them or was it just a hallucinatory trick my mind was playing on me as it sorted through its memory files?

I believe that the voices a schizophrenic hears are the same kind of voice I heard on my peyote trip. Does this mean that I experienced the so-called mental illness of a schizophrenic or does the schizophrenic have some kind of communication going on with the reality of the universe? Is the schizophrenic living in some place in his or her mind, between day-to-day reality and the reality of the universe? Are these voices the same that religious people report hearing and call the voice of God? I believe the voice or voices can only be one of three things: Either the voice is limited to the confines of the individual mind generating it for some reason, like by hallucinogenic drugs or schizophrenia, or it is the mind tuning into some form of universal knowledge by means of a frequency wave not available in normal consciousness of the mind without hallucination or schizophrenia, or it is a combination of both.

Are people who are hallucinating on drugs and schizophrenics experiencing some form of communication with universal knowledge, similar to the expansion of the mind's intelligence that Kurzweil predicts when the "singularity" happens, as explained in the last chapter?

What I take from all this is that the everyday joys and sorrows of living your life are insignificant when compared to universal reality, whatever it is. Universally, we are as insignificant as the ant is to our point of view. We want to understand (the secret of) why we are here, but have no choice except to live our everyday lives. I believe there is no concept of good and evil in the reality of the universe. Good and evil is a survival concept of humans, who must live by ethical and moral beliefs, standards and laws, to survive. To reinforce these values human beings have invented the God concept and religions to explain the unknown and give them comfort and meaning. Scientists, astronomers, and other inquiring minds know that the God concept is just another "opiate for the masses."

Dr. Michael West, deputy director for science at the Lowell Observatory in Flagstaff, Arizona, and former director of astronomy at the Maria Mitchell Association on Nantucket, wrote the following in a column titled "The Greatest Story Never Told," in the February 27, 2014 issue of *The Inquirer and Mirror*: "Right or wrong, modern science's message appears to be that we're insignificant specks in an immense purposeless universe that couldn't care less if we live or die. How inspirational can that possibly be? Few will take comfort in Nobel Laureate Steven Weinberg's view that 'The effort to understand the universe is one of the very few things that lifts human life a little above the level of farce, and gives it some of the grace of tragedy.' It's no wonder many people choose the certainty and meaning implicit in astrology or religion over science, and don't really care whether the Earth goes around the Sun or vice-versa because it's irrelevant to their daily lives. More than a century ago, the British poet and journalist Sir Edwin Arnold speculated that "It is astronomy which will eventually be the chief educator and emancipator of the human races.' But until astronomers, and scientists in general, become more adept at telling the universe's story in a way that engages the public's hearts as well as minds, science doesn't have a prayer of becoming our nation's favorite pastime. And that's a pity, because we've got the greatest story never told."

Meanwhile, the public's hearts and minds are engaged by silly situation comedies on TV like "The Big Bang Theory," and TV reality shows, with only an occasional TV greatest story like "Cosmos" or a popular science book that hardly anyone reads or understands.

I asked Dr. West how he confronts discussions with religious believers regarding the faith versus science argument. He kindly said he avoids such arguments because "I don't want to make the believers unhappy." This open-minded thinker also said, and I paraphrase, "Who knows, I may someday change my mind."

I believe that religion boxes you in until you can't think outside the box anymore. You could also substitute the word *brainwashes* for the word *boxes*. Religion brainwashes you until you can't think outside the brainwash anymore. Believers bury their heads in the sands of religion. Atheist Sam Harris, in his book *The End of Faith*, goes even further. He likened religion to a type of mental illness: "It is difficult to imagine a set of beliefs more suggestive of mental illness than those that lie at the heart of many of our religious traditions."

T.M. Luhrmann, a professor of anthropology at Stanford, stated the following opinion in an article called "Faith vs. Facts" in the *New York Times*: "A broad group of scholars is beginning to demonstrate that religious belief and factual belief are indeed different kinds of mental creatures. People process evidence differently when they think with a factual mind-set rather than with a religious mind-set. These scholars have remarked that when people consider the truth of a religious belief, what the belief does for their lives matters more than, well, the facts."

Other than with peyote and my one LSD trip, the other two times I had heavy hallucinogenic experiences were with my friends Sol Gubin in Florida and Peter Hill in Newport, both with marijuana. The peyote and LSD hallucinations were a universal out-of-body experience, while the marijuana hallucinations were in the present in-body physical realities.

My hallucinogenic episodes have given me an insight into how little we use the incredible power of the mind. I have not been given the brilliant mind of an Einstein, Hawking, Jobs, or Gates. My mind and the minds of most people are like a powerful computer sitting there with not enough powerful software to run it to its maximum capacity. Hallucination has given me a little preview of what the mind is capable of doing. I believe the marijuana acts like a mental turbocharger, which boosts your ability to think creatively.

Being born with high intelligence and acquiring great knowledge and experience is the powerful software of the mind. The brilliance of Galileo, Einstein, Stephen Hawking, and many others allowed them to look out into the universe and theorize about the reality and meaning of it all. I believe that hallucination could somehow aid in connecting your mind to the secrets of the universe. Hallucination could be some sort of preview of what we could experience if Kurzweil's "singularity" happens. It would be a kind of instant knowledge, rather than an acquired knowledge of formulas and theories. I wonder what would have happened if Einstein had experienced powerful hallucinogenic drugs. What theories would he have come up with in his incredible mind with the added stimulation of hallucinogens? Then again, he may have experienced some form of hallucination. Einstein said: "If we discover how the universe works, it will be a very simple answer." Could he have been referring to what we now call the "singularity," and the possibility of instant knowledge transmitted by frequency waves? I certainly don't believe that Einstein's simple answer will be as simple as the Bible. Most people use a computer without knowledge of the algorithms, codes, and software that make it work, which are the product of the most brilliant minds on the planet. They also use their minds without the intelligence of Einstein.

The myths of the various religions of the world have convinced me of nothing, except that they are responsible for much of the terrible state of the human condition throughout time. Marijuana has helped to free me from the bonds of religious thinking. I feel sorry for the people throughout history who lost their lives in religious wars because they disagreed with certain religious beliefs. Atheism may not be for everyone, but for me science has expanded my mind and taught me to think intelligently.

Marijuana is not for everyone either, and my intention in this book is not to try to convince anyone to use it. It has been important in my life creatively, and it has aided me greatly in expanding my mind. I do resent the bad rap it has received during my lifetime, starting with the government's anti-marijuana propaganda film *Reefer Madness*, which is a hilarious example of misinformation. Coincidentally, it was released in 1936, the year of my birth. For me, *Reefer Madness* is as untrue to the reality of what marijuana is and does, as the Bible is untrue to the reality of what the universe is and does.

As I look back from 1936 on, I feel sorry for the people who did serious jail time for possession of as little as one marijuana joint. President Obama could have ended up in jail for his admitted marijuana usage during his youth. Instead, he lucked out and became president of the United States of America. He made a comment on national news that he believes marijuana is "not as harmful as alcohol." He said he recommended his daughters stay away from marijuana, but interestingly, he didn't suggest, at least publicly, that they stay away from alcohol also.

At this stage of my life, I have given up the use of alcohol, even though I liked very good wine. I prefer to ingest a marijuana cookie whenever I choose. It safely takes my mind as far as I want to go and reduces my physical pain, while it allows me to grow intellectually. I will leave the crossing of my self-imposed safe line, between the bright and dark side of marijuana usage, to braver risk-takers and mind-travelers.

In the past few years of writing this book, there has been an accelerating increase by the states, in the number of medical marijuana clinics and in the various forms of decriminalizing and legalizing marijuana. There has been twelve times more research on the benefits of marijuana conducted in the past year than in the past twelve years combined. I am confident that as the research increases over the coming years, we will realize how truly wonderful this drug really is.

If the general population presently using alcohol, mood-altering, and pain-killing drugs discover controlled, safe, edible marijuana… sell your pharmaceutical, beer, and liquor stocks and buy marijuana stocks. Imagine marijuana TV commercials listing no side effects, if used as directed. Compare that to watching TV commercials for typical pharmaceutical prescription anti-depressant or pain killing drugs—at the end of the ad the voice-over announcer lists and disclaims the many possible side effects: diarrhea, headaches, nausea, dizziness, high or low blood pressure, liver, kidney, or heart problems and even the possibility of death.

Maybe one day soon, this will be a reality: A marijuana commercial comes on. It shows a man coming home from work. He is obviously stressed, depressed, and suffering from back, shoulder, and hip pain. He pops a 15 percent THC MariWonderWell brand marijuana capsule into his mouth. Less than one hour later, it shows him smiling and playing vigorously with his children and dog in the yard. The voice-over announcer lists the possible side effects: No pain, euphoria, happiness, intelligent thought, incredible enjoyment of the dinner his wife prepared, followed by an extremely interesting conversation about the universe with the kids. I think I would be qualified to write the jingle for this commercial. Drug companies beware.

I am certain that by the time this book is published, there will be even greater progress by the states toward legalization. Hopefully, in the next few years we will see all-out legalization in some form for medical and recreational use of marijuana by the federal government. Marijuana is in the news everywhere, almost daily. I believe it is a miracle drug and aspirin for the mind. I believe marijuana is a gateway drug, not to more serious drugs, but a gateway into expanding the mind.

Marijuana is beginning to be properly researched and discussed honestly and fairly. FINALLY ! Thank God for this. Of course I'm joking about the God part.

26

EPILOGUE: MY BIGGEST HIT

When I was ten years old and a member of the gang in my poor neighborhood, I began to realize that I was different from some of the others. Even though I liked the alpha-male leader, I felt he wasn't very smart and his leadership was based on his physical size and forceful presentation of himself. I decided that I would march through life to the beat of my own drummer. I remember thinking, *Some day I will drive back to the old neighborhood in my shiny new Cadillac and show these guys who I really am*. As my life progressed, I realized I didn't need a new car to show how successful I was and forgot about proving myself to the gang.

As I became proficient on the piano, I knew that was my life's calling. I proceeded to chase a career of pursuing stardom, hit songs, and money. Stardom eluded me, but I came to realize that I enjoyed what I was doing and was earning good money as a songwriter. While I was living a successful career in the music business, I decided that I would not continue chasing the "carrot on the stick" and living in the "rat race" of New York City. I would move my family to Vermont and live the lifestyle I really wanted. I would live like a millionaire without being one.

Vermont gave me what I wanted for my family: A beautiful house on a hill with magnificent views, privacy, no traffic, and a country lifestyle of peace and quiet. This is the place I will live out the rest of my life.

I am enjoying the biggest hits of my life: Billi, who loves me as I love her, with each other's total trust; Kristina and Erik, both of whom have healthy and successful lives; three healthy grandchildren; and a home with everything I could ever need (art, books, and media connectivity) to stimulate my creativity. I have often said, if I was ever sentenced to "house arrest," I would still be the happiest guy in the world. I do love mixing it up with the 180-degree lifestyle change of our Nantucket home. But Vermont is where my heart and soul live.

I have been fortunate to have had a successful career and am deeply grateful for it. I am thankful for the lucky breaks that I received but have become aware that, sometimes, luck is when opportunity and preparation meet.

I have learned the importance of good health and living a healthy lifestyle. Whenever I feel my aches and pains and have problems of the day, I just think about Stephen Hawking, relatives and friends who are battling cancer, newborns and children with serious health problems, and I realize how fortunate I am to have reached the age of eighty, mostly unscathed.

I wrote a song about it, "Einstein and Superman." You can check it out on YouTube.

Einstein and Superman

Do you ever wake up, not feelin' too grand
Wonderin' why you were dealt such a meaningless hand

And things seem so bad, you can't get out of bed
But it could be much worse, would you rather be dead

Chorus:
Think Stephen Hawking and Christopher Reeve
Einstein and Superman, they'll help you to believe
That things aren't ever as bad as they seem
Think Einstein and Superman, Hawking and Reeve

Life can come at you in all kinds of ways
At times it seems hopeless for days upon days
No matter how bad you think it can get
Just remember that you haven't seen nothin' yet
(*Repeat chorus*)

Whenever you think things could never get worse
And you feel like you're floatin' through the universe
Remember rule number one, 'cause there aren't any more
If you ain't havin' fun, what are you waitin' for
(*Repeat chorus*)

Billi and I are grateful for all we have and try to live according to the advice of the great ancient Chinese philosopher Lao Tzu: "Be content with what you have; rejoice in the way things are. When you realize there is nothing lacking, the whole world belongs to you."

ABOUT THE AUTHOR

Bobby Gosh has had a long and varied musical career. As a young muscican he played piano and sang in Manhattan nightclubs. While playing in Billy Reed's Little Club, Gosh met the great lyricist, Sammy Cahn and began writing songs with him, including "The Need of You," recorded by Diahann Carroll. Later, Gosh toured the world for two years as Paul Anka's pianist, orchestra conductor, and co-writer. During this time, Gosh sang and played on the original piano-voice demo of Anka's song, "My Way," which was then presented to Frank Sinatra—the rest became musical history.

Upon his return to New York City, Gosh signed recording contracts with Polydor records as well as successive ones with ABC Paramount, Capitol Records, and RCA Records. Gosh's song, "A Little Bit More," became a Top Ten hit and rock classic recorded by Dr. Hook. Many other diverse pop, rock, country, and jazz artists have also recorded Gosh's songs. Gosh's songs have been featured in several movies, including "Big," staring Tom Hanks and Woody Allen's film "Mighty Aphrodite." He also composed "Welcome to Our World of Toys," played in all FAO Schwarz stores. He has appeared as the opening act in concert with Barbra Streisand in Central Park and opened for Billy Joel at the Troubador in Hollywood.

Bobby lives in Vermont, with his wife Billi and still records songs in his state-of-the-art digital recording studio. He has two grown children, Kristina and Erik.

UNCORRECTED

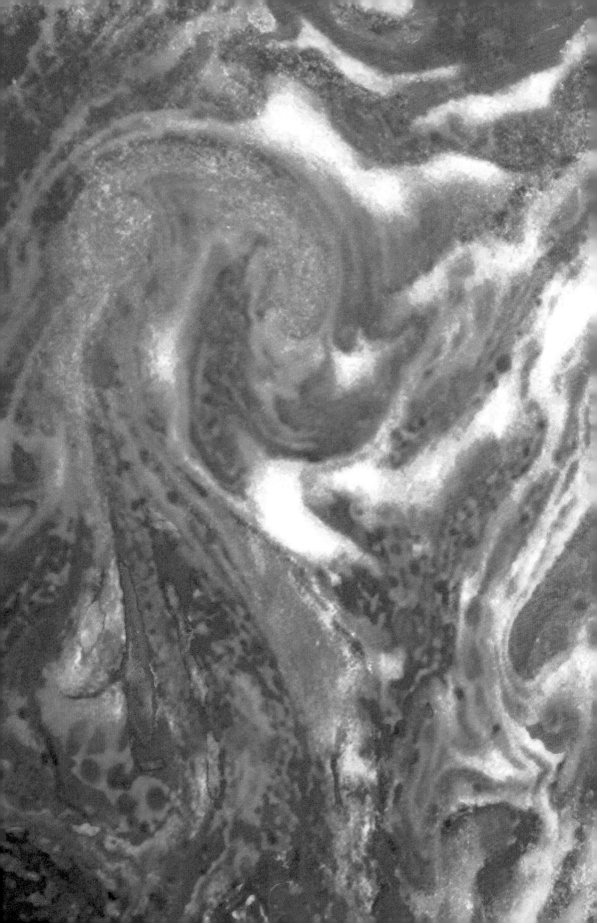

CPSIA information can be obtained
at www.ICGtesting.com
Printed in the USA
BVOW10s0616070416

443105BV00008B/8/P